D0052543

LANGUAGE AND LITERACY SERIES

Dorothy S. Strickland and Celia Genishi, SERIES EDITORS

ADVISORY BOARD: Richard Allington, Donna Alvermann,
Kathryn Au, Bernice Cullinan, Colette Daiute, Anne Haas Dyson,
Carole Edelsky, Janet Emig, Shirley Brice Heath, Connie Juel,
Susan Lytle, Timothy Shanahan

VOLUMES IN THE NCRLL SET:
APPROACHES TO LANGUAGE AND LITERACY RESEARCH

JoBeth Allen and Donna Alvermann, EDITORS

On the Case:
Approaches to Language and Literacy Research
Anne Haas Dyson and Celia Genishi

On Qualitative Inquiry:
Approaches to Language and Literacy Research
George Kamberelis and Greg Dimitriadis

ON THE CASE

Approaches to Language and Literacy Research

(AN NCRLL VOLUME)

ANNE HAAS DYSON
CELIA GENISHI

Teachers College, Columbia University
New York and London

National Conference on Research in
Language and Literacy

Published by Teachers College Press, 1234 Amsterdam Avenue, New York, NY 10027

Published in association with the National Conference on Research in Language and Literacy (NCRLL). For more about NCRLL, see *www.nyu.edu/education/ teachlearn/research/ncrll/*

Library of Congress Cataloging-in-Publication Data

Dyson, Anne Haas.
    On the case / Anne Haas Dyson and Celia Genishi.
        p. cm. — (Approaches to language and literacy research)
    (Language and literacy series) "An NCRLL volume."
    Includes bibliographical references and index.
    ISBN 0-8077-4598-7 (cloth : alk. paper). — ISBN 0-8077-4597-9 (pbk. : alk. paper)
        1. Language arts (Elementary)—Research—Methodology.
    2. English language—Social aspects. 3. Case method. I. Genishi, Celia, 1944-
    II. National Conference on Research in Language and Literacy. III. Title. IV.
    Series. V. Language and literacy series (New York, N.Y.)
    LB1576.D97 2005
    372.6'07'02—dc22   200404063685

ISBN 0-8077-4597-9 (paper)
ISBN 0-8077-4598-7 (cloth)

Printed on acid-free paper
Manufactured in the United States of America

12 11 10 09 08 07 06 05   8 7 6 5 4 3 2 1

Dedicated to our moms, lifelong child watchers,
Athleen W. Haas and,
in loving memory,
Mary Nakamura Genishi.
Their influence endures.

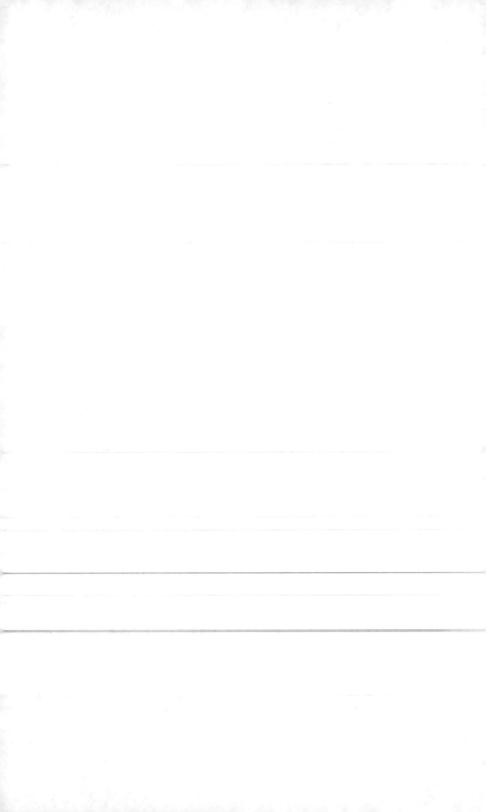

Contents

From the NCRLL Editors

D o you wish you could go back to graduate school and take more research courses? Are you in graduate school and worried that you don't have the tools to become a researcher? Does your current project cry out for an approach that you aren't quite sure how to design? Have you ever wondered how and why people study conversations in classrooms, or what different approaches there might be to case study research, or how to employ critical race theory in designing a study?

If so, you are not alone. A recent survey of the membership of the National Conference on Research in Language and Literacy (NCRLL) indicated a strong need for a comprehensive source of information about different research approaches in the field. To respond to that need, NCRLL and Teachers College Press have joined forces to develop and publish the current collection—Approaches to Language and Literacy Research. The first book, *On Qualitative Inquiry* by George Kamberelis and Greg Dimitriadis, maps the philosophical foundations and disciplinary histories of qualitative research and serves as a prelude to many of the following practice-oriented volumes. Each subsequent book, authored by one or more prominent researchers, addresses a particular research framework, tradition, or approach used by language and literacy researchers. Topics and authors tentatively slated for future volumes include Arlette Willis on research informed by critical theories; David Bloome, Nora Shuart-Faris, Stephanie Carter, Mary Beth Christian, and Sheila Otto on classroom discourse analysis; Dixie Goswami, Ceci Lewis, Marty Rutherford, Diane Waff, and Tom McKenna on teacher inquiry; Shirley Brice Heath on ethnography; David Schaafsma on narrative inquiry; David

Reinking and Barbara Bradley on formative experiments; and David Pearson on quantitative approaches.

On the Case, by Anne Haas Dyson and Celia Genishi, stitches "a quilt of persuasive images—a coherent narrative" (p. 159)—the ultimate goal of case study researchers, according to the authors. The fabric squares in this volume include intriguing classroom case studies each has conducted—Anne Haas Dyson's investigation into teaching and learning "the basics" in childhood spaces, and Celia Genishi's collaborative exploration of how young English-language learners "talk their way into print"—as well as a "case" from children's literature: the story of Peter Sis's *Madlenka* (2000), a little girl whose world is a multi-ethnic, multi-generational city block. All the children—the fictitious Madlenka as well as the real Lyron, Tionna, and Tommy—are so engaging that we hardly realize we have been led skillfully into complex theoretical and methodological aspects of case study research. By the time we reach the final chapter on why case studies matter, we already know. The children have shown us.

We believe this book, like the others in this collection, will be useful to a wide range of researchers: graduate students, novice researchers, and experienced researchers who want to learn about an unfamiliar research tradition or methodology. Each volume will address theoretical assumptions and issues within a particular tradition (including different interpretations, applications, and methods), research questions that might be addressed using that approach, design possibilities, and an annotated bibliography of exemplars. We are confident that this collection will make a major contribution to the field by connecting researchers to influential works of language and literacy scholars using a variety of approaches.

JoBeth Allen and Donna Alvermann,
NCRLL Editors

Acknowledgments

We have been "on the case" of this book for much longer than either of us initially intended. Our quick little book became a complex, collaborative endeavor. We want to acknowledge all those who helped us stay the course, especially

JoBeth Allen and Donna Alvermann, who gave us a reason to write, and Carol Collins, who gave us deadlines (subject to renegotiation); all were generous with good-humored encouragement;

"Mrs. Kay" and her young students, of Michigan, and Donna Yung-Chan and Susan Stires and their students, of New York City, who gave us rich research experiences to write about;

the Spencer Foundation, who provided each of us much appreciated support for our projects (although, of course, we are responsible for our findings and opinions);

Yanan Fan, doctoral student extraordinaire of MSU, who tamed the references, and Ida Esannason, much appreciated secretary at Teachers College, Columbia University, who typed figures meticulously and graciously; and

our students who have helped shape our ideas over the years.

A heartfelt thank you to all (and a big YIPPEE!)

CHAPTER ONE

Considering the Case: An Introduction

I n contemporary societies, schools serve children who are breathtakingly diverse in sociocultural heritage and geographic location. What, then, is the educational relevance of researchers spending vast amounts of time and always stretched institutional funds on the intense study of singular individuals, local activities, and specified places? Or, to put the same question differently, what is the use of transforming concerns about vast numbers of schoolchildren into very particular tales of individuals, activities, and places? This is the broad question that undergirds this book.

In the chapters ahead, we consider in detail what it means to be "on the case" in language and literacy studies. We consider the basic assumptions that ground a qualitative approach to case study methodology, the decisions entailed in designing a case study, and the possibilities and challenges of data collection and analysis. Through these details, we aim to clarify the unique contributions that case studies can make and have made to professional knowledge. At the same time, we aim to clarify why case studies more often complicate than comply with any public, political, or professional desires for quick fixes to educational problems.

In this first chapter, we introduce the nature and value of a case study and then discuss its theoretical underpinnings, general aims, and typical guiding questions. Within qualitative or interpretive traditions (Bogdan & Biklen, 2003; Emerson, Fretz, & Shaw, 1995; Erickson, 1986), any objective situation—a lesson, an elementary classroom, a day-care center, a community writing program or theater project—presents a plethora of potential "cases." Thus, we illustrate that cases are constructed, not found, as researchers make decisions about how to angle their vision on places overflowing with potential stories of human experience.

Throughout the chapter, we, as authors, do what we often do when we are trying to articulate complex ideas—we enlist the aid of small children. Among these children will be real ones (those who, when we knew them, were actual children) and a fictional one who lives, as does one of us, "in the universe, on a planet, on a continent, in a country, in [New York City], on a block . . ." (Sis, 2000, n. p.)

THE NATURE AND VALUE OF A CASE

In Peter Sis's book *Madlenka*, the title character is a small girl who lives on a city block. She has a loose tooth, which thrills her, and, as people do when they have news, she runs off to tell "everyone." Her "everyone" is bounded by her block but includes people from around the globe, including many shopkeepers.

Madlenka's block is not the universe "in a teacup," to echo Geertz (1973, p. 22). It *is* a teacup, so to speak. It is a small, naturalistic social unit (i.e., a social unit recognized as such by participants themselves). Through partaking in its richly brewed particulars, Madlenka makes friends (who do not have to be young, look like her, talk like her—or even have teeth); and those friends mediate her understanding of the larger world. For Madlenka, Paris is built of cakes and pies, as she sees that city through her talk with her friend the French baker. Germany is a landscape of folk creatures, as she envisions that country through the stories of an old woman, her German neighbor.

Researchers would not enter Madlenka's teacup to study the *universal biological* experience of losing a tooth or having speech. Rather, they would do so because of an interest in the *local particulars* of some abstract social phenomenon. They might wonder, for example, about the nature of a child's "everyone," that is, the people she assumes are part of her world, and how that assumed collectivity is formed and sustained through speech and other symbolic tools. They might be curious about the potential socializing role of unrelated community members who play a recurrent but circumspect role in children's lives and, at the same time, the role of unrelated children in socializing adults to potentially unfamiliar cultural practices and meanings (like being joyful about a loose tooth). In short, researchers might slip into Madlenka's teacup in order to probe the material workings of some complex and abstract aspect of human experience.

It is the messy complexity of human experience that leads researchers to case studies in the qualitative or interpretive tradition (Erickson, 1986). They identify a social unit, for example, a person, a group, a place or activity, or some combination of those units—a child's city block perhaps. That unit becomes a case of *something*, of some phenomenon; Madlenka's block might become a case of cross-generational and cross-cultural learning and of the social and language processes through which such phenomena are enacted. Through studying the details of Madlenka's experience of her block, researchers might gain insight into some of the factors that shape, and the processes through which people interpret or make meaningful, an urban landscape.

Geertz (1973) explains this interplay between the detailing of local specificity and the probing of a more abstract phenomenon. He does so by emphasizing that

> [t]he locus of study [i.e., Madlenka's block] is not the object of study [e.g., intergenerational learning]. . . . You can study different things in different places, and some things . . . you can best study in confined localities. . . . It is with the kind of material produced by long-term . . . highly participative, and almost obsessively fine-comb study in confined contexts that the megaconcepts with which contemporary social science is af-

flicted . . . can be given the sort of sensible actuality that makes it possible to think not only realistically and concretely *about* them, but, what is more important, creatively and imaginatively with them. (p. 23)

Any detailed "case" (e.g., a studied teacher's pedagogy, a child's learning history) is just that—a case. It is not the phenomenon itself (e.g., effective teaching, writing development). That phenomenon may look and sound different in different social and cultural circumstances, that is, in different cases. This relationship between a grand phenomenon and mundane particulars suggests key theoretical assumptions of qualitative case studies, particularly those involving the production of *meaning* and its dependence on *context*.

THEORETICAL ASSUMPTIONS

What is the meaning of a loose tooth? Or, to phrase the question differently, how is a loose tooth made meaningful? In Sis's (2000) book, Madlenka's loose tooth causes no pain, only joy and an urge to spread the news about this special happening. Indeed, it is an occasion for a sugary treat from Mr. Ciao's ice cream truck! Thus, Madlenka's loose tooth is made meaningful by how she represents or symbolizes that experience and by the emotions she associates with the experience (i.e., by her joyful shouting) and, also, by how others respond to and join in to celebrate with her. Madlenka is becoming a "big girl"!

The situation of a loose tooth means something quite different in Mrs. Kay's and Ms. Hache's first-grade classroom in a Midwestern city. It is dental week, and the children have just watched a video featuring a talking tooth. That tooth describes the life experiences of baby teeth—when they grow in, when they fall out, and what happens if they do not receive proper care. Six-year-old Tionna is critical of this video. There was, she points out, no blood; the baby tooth was "supposed to be bleeding" when it came out. A discussion of wiggling and bleeding follows and then one on family members—uncles and fathers especially—whose "yucky" teeth went from white, to yellow, to brown and black and, finally, to falling out. And, Lyron stresses, these people are "grown ups[!]", not 6-year-olds with baby teeth.

As Madlenka, Tionna, and Lyron make clear, people produce meaning in their lives in part by how they use shared symbol systems for representing objects, actions, and other people (Hall, 1997). Chief among these systems is language (Vygotksy, 1962). We appropriate words from a shared linguistic repertoire to name and narrate our experiences. In this way, language is both a repository of cultural meanings and a medium for the production of meaning in everyday life.

Moreover, as the children also demonstrate, an object (or a person) does not have a fixed meaning. A loose tooth may be responded to as a biological indicator of human growth, a personally painful and bloody experience, an occasion for celebration and treats, and even (as Tionna and her classmates eventually discuss) an opportunity for economic gain (through the tooth fairy, assuming she knows where the tooth's owner is sleeping). Thus, the ways people represent and interact about experiences, like having a loose tooth, depend on more than a shared repertoire for meaning making. They also depend on the contexts—the frameworks for interpretation—that people bring to those experiences.

On Physical Settings and Social Events

"Context" itself is a complex concept, whose meaning is not fixed (Goodwin & Duranti, 1992). In one sense, context is the physical setting of people's actions. For Madlenka, it is a city block; for Tionna, it is a public school classroom.

In language and literacy studies, researchers view those settings as themselves constituted by social activities. Hymes (1972a), an ethnographer of communication, used the term "speech events" to refer to those activities that are structured by ways of talking. Such events would include, for example, ways of greeting others, telling stories, playing, praying, and even teaching (Mehan, 1982). Other scholars (Basso, 1974; Heath, 1983) expanded language events to include "literacy events"—social activities structured around ways of using (and talking about) text. In fact, activities involving oral language provide contexts for most instances of print use: "Even in the most seemingly literate of environments, such as the law court, a schoolroom, or a university office, most of the conventions of how to act and what to do [with and through texts] are passed on orally" (Barton, 1994, p. 90).

Different kinds of events are energized by different purposes; are characterized by particular relationships among participants; and are marked by expected moods, by possible and anticipated interactions, and by expected topics and structures. Researchers have investigated the diverse ways in which such events are organized within the flow of everyday life in particular settings.

In the very beginnings of qualitative research on classroom language, researchers focused on particular social participants in school (a child, a group of children, members of particular sociocultural groups) and followed them across language events involving, for example, different ways of grouping children, of organizing speaking turns, of using varied languages and registers. They were interested in how factors of culture, class, and language figured into school failure (e.g., Cazden, Hymes, & John, 1972).

Within their cases, these researchers demonstrated that "personal" qualities like being talkative, literate, or even logical in language use were socially interpreted responses to situations (e.g., Carrasco, Vera, & Cazden, 1981; Diaz, Moll, & Mehan, 1986; Labov, 1972; Philips, 1975). Many contextual factors matter in how children use language, among them the assumed purpose for communicating, the demographic qualities of participants (e.g., age, gender, culture, social class), the implicit rules governing the right to speak, and the language and dialect being used.

On the day Madlenka's tooth becomes loose, she steps out onto her city block, itself filled with people with whom she has a history of shared conversations and storytelling events. With her voice and, indeed, her body she invokes a celebratory context as she moves around the block, seeking out friends with whom to share her news. She exuberantly yells, jumps, and skips. One imagines that, in a classroom, she might not yell across the physical setting, "Hey, everyone! My tooth is loose!"

And of course, Madlenka's actions are coordinated with others, who respond with interest to the news of this little girl and offer appropriate congratulations. Language events are collaboratively constructed; participants must understand one another's obligations, given the nature of the event and their respective roles and statuses. In Madlenka's case, participants join in a pleasant conversational encounter. Their cultural differences (related to age, language, ethnic heritage) do not interfere with the production of meaning but, to the contrary, enrich it, or, at the very least, enrich Madlenka's imaginative worlds. As Bakhtin (1981) might say, participants accept their responsibility to answer one another.

In their classroom lesson event, Tionna and her classmates first listen to an instructional video. They are to learn facts from this video (despite its cartoon figures). During the class discussion that follows, they (for the most part) do not yell out but raise their hands to report what they have learned. Still, the children do speak up in their class when they "have a problem" with a text (or a film), to quote Janette, another child. And their problems sometimes reveal the interpretative frames they bring from their own experiences—baby teeth bleed, adults lose teeth. Their experiences go beyond the information given, as do contexts themselves.

On Cultural Practices and Societal Structures

More recently, researchers have used the term "cultural practices" to refer to recurrent kinds of events. The concept of a "practice" emphasizes the ways in which everyday events "come packed with values about what is natural, mature, morally right, or aesthetically pleasing" (Miller & Goodnow, 1995,

p. 6). As children come to participate and to interact within the shared practices of a group of people, they develop a sense of identity and of belonging to that group. At the same time, the very ways of interacting that may be deemed appropriate and even necessary within particular groups may be deemed immature (i.e., not fully developed), morally problematic, or simply unpleasant by others.

The concept of a practice, with its explicit emphasis on identity and ideologies (assumptions about values, ideas, and relationships between people), is a link to another conception of context. In addition to the physical setting and invoked and co-constructed event or practice, there is also the "extrasituational context" (Goodwin & Duranti, 1992, p. 8). That context is the larger ethnographic one, including the historical, economic, and cultural forces that intersect in any local space (Gupta & Ferguson, 1997). These powerful forces are articulated in the unfolding interaction as well, as they inform who speaks, what gets said, and the sort of public meaning that gets established (Bakhtin, 1981). The French philosopher Michel Foucault's concept of discourses (i.e., ways of talking, including actual terms and statements) captures this link between power and public meaning or "truth" (Foucault, 1980).

In Madlenka's story, the world articulated is one in which neighborhoods are welcoming places for children, cultural diversity gives rise to joyful learning, and loose teeth yield celebrations, although there is that old woman whose lost teeth are not narrativized, or placed within the context of a story.

Lost teeth are narrativized in the vignette from Tionna's and Lyron's classroom—one of many differences from Madlenka's story. Tionna and her classmates are culturally diverse (although certainly not as much so as Madlenka's friends), but that diversity is seldom explicitly articulated in the official life of their classroom, nor do they and their teachers seem to have a shared language—a discourse—for that purpose. The children's school faces out to a commercialized stretch of neighborhood, but it is designed for adults desiring inexpensive items and varied kinds of services (including day laborers who congregate hoping for work). Bad teeth, like old shoes and coats with broken zippers, are one potential correlate of socioeconomic troubles, and although those correlates were not mentioned in the film, they were at least suggested in what the children themselves had to say on the topic of teeth.

The ways in which people make a loose tooth meaningful are shaped by context and that context can refer to, for example, a commercialized big city block or to an elementary classroom; to an informal conversation or a formal health lesson; and to the larger economic, cultural, and historical forces that shape and are shaped by local encounters. What a loose tooth means depends upon setting, event, and discursive conditions.

In their case studies, qualitative researchers are interested in the meaning people make of their lives in very particular contexts. They "combine close analysis of fine details of behavior and meaning in everyday social interaction with analysis of the wider societal context—the field of broader social influences"—within which their everyday interactions take place (Erickson, 1986, p. 120). Whether they are studying children learning to read, or to write, or to talk in a first language or a second, researchers assume that learners and their teachers make sense of talk and text within physical settings and through social activities that are informed by the world beyond the visible one. Everyday teaching and learning are complex social happenings, and understanding them as such is the grand purpose of qualitative case studies.

GENERAL AIMS AND TYPICAL QUESTIONS

To illustrate the general aims and typical questions of qualitative case studies, we begin with a hypothetical research example that is inconsistent with those aims and inappropriate in its questions. Imagine a researcher who has been intrigued by young children's often intense involvement with the popular media (the phenomenon of interest). As luck would have it, she has a friend who teaches a first–second grade combination class in a nearby city school. With her friend's blessings, the researcher enters the classroom, tape recorder in tow. Her friend's classroom is her "case." One by one, she pulls class members aside and asks each to name three favorite television shows and three favorite movies and then to provide reasons for the choices. The researcher's records indicate that the question about reasons elicited some shoulder shrugs and "I don't know's." Nonetheless, she analyzes the interplay between grade (first, second) and child taste in television and movies. She even writes a report on a "case study of first- and second-grade children's media show preferences"—a paper that is *not* a case study in the interpretive tradition.

The problems with the study do not necessarily include using a friend's classroom. But the apparent aims of the project and its implied questions (about the relationship between two variables, age and media taste) are not appropriate for qualitative case studies. The aim of such studies is not to establish relationships between variables (as in experimental studies) but, rather, to see what some phenomenon means as it is socially enacted within a particular case. For example, the researcher might wonder (as did one of us) not only what media the children attend to but also how children use their media experiences as they participate in the official and unofficial (child-governed) events of this classroom.

Just as one can ask how losing a tooth is made meaningful, one can ask how the media are made meaningful in a particular social unit or case. How do young children "do" being media participants in their class? How do they incorporate it into their talk, play, drawing, and writing in varied language events? How are their perceptions of one another—and their teacher's perceptions of them—mediated by this displayed involvement with the media? How does what's going on in the classroom relate to larger levels of social organization? For example, how do children's use and response to media texts help construct or interrupt larger societal structures (e.g., class, race, and gender, as well as age)?

In a similar way one can ask, How does one do being a "deaf child" in a classroom (Ramsey, 1997), an "English-language learner" (Genishi, Yung-Chan, & Stires, 2000; Meyer, Klein, &

Genishi, 1994), or a "popular girl" in a junior high English class (Finders, 1997)? In a case study, any descriptor that might be attached to a child (e.g., *literate, struggling, proficient, ELL,* or *ESL*) becomes a socially accomplished construct enacted in particular physical settings, in certain kinds of events or practices, and with particular materials and is infused with certain ideologies or assumptions about how the world works. A powerful illustration of this notion is provided by Padden and Humphries (1988). They discuss a Deaf child in a Deaf family who was not aware that he was "different" until he entered into the institution of the school:

> Now deafness becomes a prominent fact in his life, a term around which people's behavior changes. People around him have debates about deafness, and lines are sharply drawn between people depending on what position they take on the subject. He has never thought about himself as having a certain quality, but now it becomes something to discuss. Even his language has ceased to be just a means of interacting with others and has become an object: people are either "against" signed language or "for" signed language. In the stories we have collected from Deaf children of Deaf parents, the same pattern emerges over and over: "Deafness" is "discovered" late and in the context of these layers of meaning. (p. 18)

Given this emphasis on meaning perspectives and contexts, the aims of qualitative research are not compatible with efforts to identify the "scientifically proven" teaching methods that will cure children of language or literacy ills and ensure all a healthy literacy future in school (for a quite explicit use of a medical approach to education, see *www.NoChildLeftBehind. org*). Singular case studies do not aim to determine context-free associations between methodological input and achievement data. Indeed, there is no thermometer with which to take a child's literacy temperature, nor to check that a child's English proficiency is within the normal range.

In this research approach, then, there is no assumption that teaching methods per se are causal; indeed, particular teaching approaches that work in one setting may not work in another (Dyson, 1993; Reyes, 1992), and those that work with one child may not work with another (Chittenden, Salinger, & Bussis, 2001; Genishi, Dubetz, & Focarino, 1995). What are causal are human interpretations, on the basis of which people act. Both teachers and students bring interpretive frames that influence their ways of attending and responding to others within the social activities of the classroom. The researcher uses particular methods of observation and analysis to understand *others'* understandings (their sense of what's happening and, therefore, what's relevant) and the processes through which they enact language and literacy education.

ANGLED VISIONS AND CONSTRUCTED CASES

Any educational setting—a classroom, a school, a family, a community program—is overflowing with human experiences and with human stories. Researchers make decisions about how to angle their vision on these places, depending on the interplay between their own interests and the grounded particularities of the site. Madlenka, for example, might have been a minor character in a study of that elderly German neighbor, who experiences the city block primarily through the view from her window. What and whom does she see as she looks out her window? What does she make of the children she sees? Who are the children she talks with? What does New York City mean to her, as she understands it, through knowing children?

In the remainder of this chapter, we allow a brief glimpse into two different research sites. Each has the potential to give rise to the study of varied phenomena through varied case studies of particular people, particular kinds of practices, particular kinds of classrooms, or a combination of these. The first scene below comes from Lyron and Tionna's classroom.

Scene 1: Mrs Kay's First Grade (Anne)

On this day, Ms. Hache, the student teacher, has read and talked with the first graders about the Pilgrims' arduous trip from England to Plymouth. She now gives each child a "packet," a set of pictures to color. Today they are to color only the first two pages.

As the children color, Ms. Hache circulates, commenting to this or that child about the appearance of the sky and the color of the water or of the sails of the new boats, just setting out on their journeys.

As researcher, I have been sitting off to the side of the class, but now that "the lesson" is becoming a collage of conversations, it is time for me to make a move. I settle in by Lyron, one of the focal (or regularly observed) children in a case study of peer culture and literacy "basics" in this class (i.e., how children individually and collectively respond to the identified basic skills). Being with Lyron entails being with any child in his hailing range. Right now, in fact, he is hailing a male friend and excitedly calling out the dramatic action on his page. Lyron is not just coloring. He has drawn people on top of the *Mayflower*. They are Pilgrims jumping into the water! "And I can pretend the Pilgrims are going to eat the octopuses up," since "it's salt water with octopuses in it."

"Well, why not?" I think. The Pilgrims, Lyron knows, run short of food. Although octopi do not hang out in the middle of the ocean, Lyron has situated the Pilgrim scene in the center of an action-packed audiovisual adventure (a familiar tack for him). Thus he has slipped from a world presented as "factual" into one that is much more animated—a "pretend" one in which given facts can be taken as an invitation for dramatic play (at least until Ms. Hache notices the drawing and requests that it stop).

I have entered now, as best I can, into the experiential world of this first-grade classroom and, more specifically, into the worlds of particular children. The project is new, my focus still quite general, but I find myself pulled into a familiar narrative line (e.g., Dyson, 1984, 2003). I am detailing the official communicative practices of this classroom, which is located in a school under pressure to teach the "basics" (e.g., learning to compose brief texts, spell conventionally, use basic text mechanics, edit for grammatical usage). I wonder how such practices organize children's social ends and symbolic actions (drawing, writing, talking), about their points of vulnerability for child agency, and about their consequences for how child-hoods themselves are constructed in and through school.

However, instead of angling her vision in this classroom to spotlight the children, a researcher could foreground the teachers' enactment of their roles, particularly when and how they enforce a "standard," a uniformity in children's responses (e.g., one colors but does not add little drawings to one's study "packet"). *Uniformity* is not a word used by the teachers, and so one project aim could be to develop a locally informed vocabulary that captures the nuances of expected child responses.

Another potential case study might be of holidays as curricular focal points and enacted school events. What is the meaning of traditional holidays in a classroom serving children from diverse sociocultural heritages? How do children and teachers talk about holidays and their symbols? What roles do adults and children play in articulating the public meaning of holidays? In such a case study, the researcher would focus on neither teacher nor child. Rather, she would focus on particular classroom and even schoolwide events, since holidays provide the motivational and substantive content for much official talk, reading, and writing.

WIDENING THE ANGLE IN CASE CONSTRUCTION

The act of angling one's vision, then, may not always follow a singular decision. In most cases the decision is negotiated, informed by the individuals, educational program, and local politics of a research site. So a researcher might at first expect to focus on children in one room and their understanding of holidays, but later decide to make the school building the case, as a consequence of observing in and around the children's spaces. In this sense the decision about how to angle one's vision is collaborative, and how narrow or wide the angle is depends on a mix of what's going on at the site and the preferences and strengths of a researcher or researchers. The question that guided the study at the start (what are the children's understandings of holidays?) evolves into a few questions that are better answered by widening the angle of the researcher's lens, by adding questions: What are the adults' understandings? How does the community around the school influence these understandings? How do holidays fit into the curriculum of a particular classroom? Thus, a topic that might seem straightforward or hackneyed comes to life because of greater knowledge of a site and a resulting decision to change research lenses.

A topic that is seldom straightforward or hackneyed, because of the growing diversity of children in many sites around the world, is that of language learning. In North America the language being learned is most often English, and the presence of children who enter classrooms speaking a language other than English is on the rise (U.S. Department of Education, 2003). Indeed, in many urban areas Madlenka would find herself in the company of children whose ethnic heritage is as varied as that of the population on her block. In contrast, in some neighborhoods and classrooms, children share one language that is not English, for example, Chinese or Spanish. In their classrooms there is the audible complexity of multiple languages, with a teacher often speaking English. If we invite Madlenka to step out of the pages of her imagined world, how would she fare in a classroom where children spoke multiple languages different from her own or a language not her own? How would she share the excitement of her loose tooth?

Of course, the answers vary, depending on the locale in which she finds herself. As an English speaker in North America, she would be privileged; she would speak the teacher's language and the "target language," the one children are encouraged to learn, often as quickly as possible. Madlenka herself might not notice her privileged status, though, because on her tour of schools, children in the classroom she visits first are speaking Chinese, a language that, for her, is a set of mysterious sounds that are as mysterious as those of English for her new peers. Still, she and they quickly draw on resources that adults and children often use without much thought: gestures like pointing and smiles and other facial expressions that communicate as well as conventional words. And, capitalizing on what they know, some children supplement nonverbal means with non-English words they use with their families. The words may not be understood by everyone, but the intentions behind them often are.

Scene 2: Ms. Yung's Pre-Kindergarten (Celia)

Like Madlenka on leave from her book world, a few years ago I entered a classroom in which almost all the children started the school year speaking a Chinese language, Cantonese, Mandarin, or Fujianese. In Donna Yung-Chan's public school pre-kindergarten, any visitor would be surrounded not only by children as they chose, engaged in, or departed from activities, but also by their and the teacher's talk (Genishi, Yung-Chan, & Stires, 2000). In a collaborative study of how children learned English in this classroom, it was convenient at first to call the classroom the "case." My angle on this case needed to be wide enough to take in the children; Donna, their teacher; Rose Anne, the assistant teacher; and other adults who had professional or visitor roles, including coresearcher and staff developer Susan Stires. In fact, the angle shifted so that it sometimes narrowed to focus on individual English-language learners or on the teacher and her assistant with children. Because these two adults spoke most of the English heard by the children, especially at the beginning of the school year, they were viewed as key players in the complicated story of how the children became English speakers and how they began to read the world of their classroom.

In many ways a classroom of English-language learners is similar to any other classroom, but in other ways it is remarkably different. Here many children are constructing—in concert with others—a locally-informed vocabulary, plus global aspects of a new language, at the same time that they are expected to learn content in that new language. For example, there is school- or agency-mandated pressure on children, even pre-kindergarten children, to demonstrate some knowledge of conventional literacy (Snow, Burns, & Griffin, 1998). Imagine what it must be like for a 4-year-old Chinese speaker to respond to this pressure in a room in which all children are required to engage in learning the "letter of the week" in English. In fact, Donna, the teacher in my study classroom, was ever conscious of pressures like this, but folded in her own conversational "exercises," like the following, to help children develop knowledge of letters of the alphabet (example drawn from data related to Genishi et al., 2000):

> DONNA: Can you find your name card? Very good! . . .
>   What letter is this? (Repeats question in Cantonese)
> BRIAN: A.
> DONNA: What letter is this? This is I, I. Can you say it for
>   me?
> BRIAN: I.
> DONNA: Want to say for me? What's this? B.
> BRIAN: (Spelling with Donna) B-R-I-A-N! (Repeats letters
>   faster, with Donna)
> DONNA: Whose name is that? (Repeats question in Cantonese)
> BRIAN: Brian!
> DONNA: Brian, I like the way you write your name.

This Q-and-A mini-lesson occurred in the last 3 months of the school year, after many children had begun to speak more English than Brian did. Donna has a conversation with him, like many earlier conversations she has had, which meets the spirit of a school district guideline to introduce children to the fundamentals of reading and writing. Yet she avoids the rigidity of a mandate, for example, that of Head Start programs requiring all children to learn 10 letters by the end of the pre-kindergarten year (Head Start Bureau, 2003) and draws instead on as many resources as she can, including her fluency in Cantonese and Brian's fascination with his own name.

We researchers viewed the action in this room through multiple lenses. Most often our lens framed at least two people, and Donna was often in the picture. After reading and re-reading field notes and viewing and reviewing videotapes and transcripts based on those tapes, we realized that we had been on multiple cases: Sometimes we were on the case of someone like Brian and at other times—through a lens with a very wide angle—we turned out to be on the case of Donna's curriculum. This was a retrospective and abstract construction that incorporated many other cases. From our collective angle of vision, as a set of planned and unplanned enactments related to broad learning goals, that set constituted Donna's curriculum.

In short, there are many potential paths of inquiry along which researchers angle their vision to look at multiple phenomena of interest. One never simply observes a classroom. The "classroom" itself is a gloss for a complex dynamic among people. A researcher adopts a position that highlights certain elements of classroom life and lets other elements become the backdrop—the context, as it were—for the characters and events starring in the unfolding case.

SUMMARY: ON IMAGINED WORLDS

Madlenka lives only in our imaginations. She is not "real." And yet the line between the "real" and the "imagined" is not so firmly set. Loose teeth, like sailing ships, deafness, literacy, and language proficiency, do not have a fixed meaning. Rather, adults and children interpret their meanings in particular situations through interactions with others. And just as those adults and children are interpreting their experiences, so too may researchers who are studying them. Through collecting observations, talking with other people, and collecting artifacts, case study researchers aim to enter into other people's "imaginative universes" (Geertz, 1973, p. 13). That is, they aim to construct interpretations of other people's interpretations— of others' "real worlds." In the chapters ahead, we examine in more detail the methods through which this is done as we continue on the case.

CHAPTER 2

Casing the Joint:
The Social Dimensions and
Dynamics of Educational Sites

C lifford Geertz (1996, p. 262) writes, "No one lives in the world in general. Everybody, even the exiled, the drifting, the diasporic, or the perpetually moving, lives in some confined and limited stretch of it—'the world around here.'" As detailed in Chapter 1, as case study researchers, we are interested in how children, teachers, and other educational participants experience the world around them. What is it like to be a teacher, a learner, and a user of language and languages in particular places?

It is not so easy, however, to gain access to others' worlds. Before researchers have decided on their case, they may have only a general interest in some phenomenon in some potential physical sites—a neighborhood, a school, a classroom, a play-ground, or a city block, perhaps. It takes literal time, as well as methodological work, to understand how such sites are rendered meaningful places by the people who live there.

To begin this work, researchers "case the joint," so to speak. That is, situated on the edge of local action, they slowly but deliberately amass information about the configuration of time and space, of people, and of activity in their physical sites. Such information will allow them to transform general questions and interests about the phenomena they are curious about into particular and answerable questions. Moreover, it will help them make informed decisions about project design, that is, about what documents to collect and what people and activities to observe and interview.

In this chapter, we consider the processes and procedures involved in casing the joint. We consider primarily those situations in which researchers are relative strangers in unfamiliar sites. Researchers, of course, may turn an analytic eye to their own everyday worlds in classrooms and schools, aiming to gain some distance from those taken-for-granted worlds. Nonetheless, the same techniques of deliberately mapping out time, space, people, and activity can help in this process. In the sections to come, then, we consider the kinds of information that researchers initially gather and, further, the conceptual tools they use to help them approach educational sites as socially organized places for language use. We will draw on our own research processes to illustrate how a general interest in a phenomenon becomes grounded in particulars. We will close with some practical suggestions for the record-keeping procedures researchers may use to document their work.

CONFIGURING SPACE AND TIME

Imagine a researcher interested in informal intergenerational learning in a densely populated urban area. That researcher would have to know about times and spaces that present opportunities for such learning. The researcher begins, perhaps, by visiting schools in an urban area and talking with children about the people they know in their neighborhoods. Maybe the children draw maps of places they go to on their blocks, adding pictures of the people they know (rather like the picture book featuring Madlenka). As the researcher talks informally with children about their maps, she also begins visiting neighborhoods. In this way, she gets a sense of where and when children move out into their city blocks and, moreover, of which children have opportunities for intergenerational conversations beyond their family unit. The researcher is thus preparing to make informed decisions about project design for formal data collection.

In similar ways, case study researchers precede formal data collection with amassing basic information about space, time, and people in some site or sites. Some of this information can come from varied kinds of documents. Curricular documents from state departments of education, district offices, and school sites themselves, as well as federal policy guidelines, help situate schools within institutional space (i.e., within a multilayered hierarchy of expectations and evaluations). Local newspapers help situate schools within community discourses about public schools and neighborhoods, which themselves can be illuminated by Websites providing census and school population data (e.g., *http://nces.ed.gov*).

Still, the bulk of the work of casing the joint happens in early visits to sites themselves. We suggest procedures for casing a joint below.

Maps

Even when educational case studies are located in classrooms, researchers pay attention to the physical layout of schools themselves, as well as to the surrounding neighborhood. For them, it may matter where classrooms are located (e.g., in outside portable buildings, basements, first or second floors) and where they are positioned (e.g., relative to other grade levels, libraries, and even restrooms). In some schools, for example, special reading classes or English as a second language classes may be held in corners of hallways or in redone closets, which is at least suggestive of their relationship to the main agenda of the schools.

Tionna and Lyron's first-grade classroom was located on the first floor of an old building built in the early 1900s. To get to the boys' and girls' restrooms, children needed to go down the first-floor hall, through huge double doors, down a twisting staircase to the basement, and through another long hall. (The drinking fountain, fortunately or unfortunately, was located on the first floor, across from their classroom.) This restroom placement accounted, in part, for the more frequent use of gendered language in their classroom, relative to other classrooms in which we have worked, all of which had sinks and bathrooms in or nearby their classroom. When the class went to the restrooms, the teacher lined up "boys wanting to use the restroom," "drinks-only people" (girls and boys who only wanted to use the water fountain), and "girls wanting to use the restroom." The teacher arranged and monitored these separate groupings in a complex act of orchestration, which also entailed monitoring solo bathroom visits throughout the day and, therefore, which and how many boys and girls were out of the room.

Other schools, usually referred to as "suburban," may consist of a sprawling, one-story building from which everyone can see greenery through the many windows. Young children in these schools often have bathrooms and water sources within the classroom space, and they bring their own lunches. In a range of schools, lunch also happens within the classroom of the youngest children, making the orchestration of lines and corridor walks unnecessary. The extent of monitoring and use of "management language" are dramatically lower in these classrooms than in Tionna and Lyron's room.

Within the classroom itself, researchers may note the arrangement of children's seating, the location of children's individual possessions, and the placement of shared classroom supplies. For example, supplies like pencils, markers, and paste may be in a central shared location or distributed among individual children. The former situation may engender relatively more talk involving managing resources and, in the process, managing relationships (e.g., who shares what with whom).

The spatial distribution of library and reference materials, along with any computer or other electronic equipment, matters as well. Are they within reach of children as well as teachers? Are they in designated areas in the classroom or in other locations (e.g., computer rooms)? What kind of materials are on the walls? Are they: commercially prepared, teacher-made, or child-made?

Initial maps of school and classroom space are useful not only in and of themselves but also, potentially, as data-collection tools. For example, researchers may be interested in how students arrange themselves in those times of day when they control seating. During formal data collection, class maps can be duplicated and used for quick jottings of children's daily seating locations. Those same maps could be used to trace teachers' movements as they monitor or circulate among students. It is through such arrangements and movements that spaces become places for teachers' and children's school lives.

Schedules

In addition to configurations of space, researchers may gather initial information about the official configuration of time. What is the daily schedule of activities? That schedule may not be followed, but it is important nonetheless. As a text, it mediates a range of conflicting pressures and goals, emanating from varied institutional sources. For example, while some aspects of the schedule may be set by state or district requirements (e.g., the number of minutes per day spent on this subject or that), other aspects may be set by school logistics (e.g., times and days to use computer lab or playground).

Of those subjects or activities scheduled by the teacher, some may be set for mornings, others for afternoons; some may be daily, others every other day or weekly. Time for activities set for late in the morning or afternoon may be regularly reduced, as lunch or the end-of-the-day bell arrives unrelentingly at the appointed hour (and late children may miss the bus, which has its own schedule to keep). In Lyron and Tionna's room, children's independent writing was scheduled for the last 45 minutes of the day; writing itself involved a series of activities, the last of which was whole-class sharing. Sharing was often rushed, with each child getting a quick turn to read their writing before the trips to the hall lockers and, in winter, the laborious process of zipping up, pulling on, and tugging down began. There were complex institutional and pedagogical meanings undergirding the teacher's scheduling decisions, but those would be uncovered only over time. In the beginning of a project, a researcher just begins to sense the routines of time and space and the characters they involve.

People

Space and time are organized by, and organize, participants' actions (i.e., their intentional behavior). Indeed, in the preceding discussion, we have used descriptions of participants' verbal and nonverbal behavior to illustrate how space and time became meaningful. In this section, we focus specifically on means for gaining some initial insight into the social organization of people in a research setting.

To begin, researchers must learn the names of participants. In early childhood and elementary classrooms especially, researchers may learn students' names by listening (helpfully supplemented by referring to a class roll). In this way, they minimize their own roles as participants and work to keep themselves at the edge of classroom life (a topic to which we will return in Chapter 3).

Demographic qualities of classroom participants also matter, since race, ethnicity, gender, socioeconomic situation and linguistic competence may all figure in significant ways into the meaningfulness of classroom life. Initial judgments about these matters are always tentative. Parents may have indicated ethnicity or race on school enrollment forms. Socioeconomic circumstance can be roughly indexed by whether children qualify for the federal lunch program.

Over time, researchers may learn how students define themselves and others in the local situation. In one of our projects (Dyson, 2003), a child whose mother was White and whose father was Chinese declared herself African American. Given that the dominant categories in her school were "White" and "African American," she deemed herself "African American," which, to her, meant that she was not White.

The distinction between etic, or researcher-introduced, ways of naming key categories and dimensions of experience, and emic ways used by participants is critically important (a distinction attributed to Pike; see Geertz, 1973). For our purposes here, it helps articulate the connection between casing the joint, or gaining initial insights into the social organization of a research site, and the more formal data collection and analysis necessary to understand how participants themselves name and organize their world. This distinction is central to understanding initial ways of attending to the social organization of language use in a site.

THE SOCIAL DYNAMICS OF LANGUAGE USE

In this section, we consider how researchers use basic concepts from sociolinguistics or, more particularly, the ethnography of communication (introduced in Chapter 1) to begin to pay attention to sites as places for language use. Educational sites can seem a blur of human energy or, conversely, a dull march through familiar terrain (e.g., reading lessons, spelling tests). Sociolinguistic tools can help researchers gain some sense of how social activity organizes—and is organized by—time, space, and human action. In language and literacy studies, researchers are particularly interested in social activities as organized by language use, that is, in speech and literacy events and practices (see Chapter 1).

It will take immersion in settings over time to understand what and how particular events matter to the people involved, including any local or emic labels for social events and any discourses evoked when particular events are discussed (e.g., of gender, ability, social class). Initially, though, etic language (for example, "events" and "participation structures") allow researchers to use the scholarly traditions and conceptual tools of others who have studied the social organization of human activity, including teaching and learning.

Recall, for example, that imagined researcher who was interested in intergenerational learning. She has been visiting neighborhoods trying to figure out where and how to situate her study, that is, how to bound it in a case. She is going to spend a few days this week on the block mentioned by the very talkative Madlenka ("potentially good informant," she has noted in her field book). As she settles in at one of the block's shops for an hour-long observation (in the latter half of the afternoon—prime time on a weekday, she has already realized), she pulls out a little pad. She is going to take quick jottings on the nature of the shopkeeper's exchanges with customers. Considering each encounter an event (and informed by Hymes's [1972a] discussion of the components of a speech event), she notes who is involved in each encounter (e.g., how many participants, approximate ages), the event's apparent purpose, communication channels used (e.g., language spoken, any use of written language such as ads, coupons, receipt), the topic of the talk, the mood of the encounter, and any apparent interactive routines (e.g., "Hi, [name]. [pause] Did you find everything? [pause] That's 5 dollars and 41 cents. [pause] Thank you. [pause] Plastic OK? [Pause] Have a nice day.").

From this kind of quick jotting on a couple of days, the researcher can draw no conclusions, but she may begin to get a sense of the nature of intergenerational learning opportunities in a community as they unfold in the out-of-school lives of young urban children like Madlenka and in the workdays of small commercial establishments. She might begin to make decisions about how to design her formal study, including about the precise nature of the case itself.

The researcher might decide to bound her study in the experiences of the child Madlenka, observing her in many different kinds of intergenerational events in varied times and places. Or perhaps she decides to bound her study in the experiences of a shopkeeper, like the greengrocer Mr. Eduardo, observing his interactions with a range of children and young people, maybe developing a kind of taxonomy of intergenerational events. The researcher might even decide to bound her study within the block itself, collecting examples of the activity of intergenerational learning wherever she documents it as she moves around the block.

Similarly, a classroom can be thought of as a series of social events, linked by varied and more loosely organized transitional times. The school day might start with a morning meeting time (itself composed of varied events, like checking the calendar, sharing stories from home, and hearing a teacher-read story). It then might flow into a series of reading-lesson events, followed by a bathroom and drink break and a recess break, and then writing-lesson events (which themselves might proceed from teacher-led modeling, to individual children's simultaneous writing events, to one-to-one editing sessions involving a teacher and a child, and, finally, a group sharing time).

Just as the researcher did on Madlenka's block, a researcher in a classroom might make quick jottings on these varied events. Who participates in what events? What is their ostensible purpose? What generally is talked about? What is the prevailing mood? What languages are used? What texts are discussed? What is the nature of the participation structure (Philips, 1972) of these events? That is, how is interaction organized? For example, some events involve the whole class, others are in small-group formats, still others involve children sitting side by side but doing individual tasks. For many events, the teacher determines who speaks when, but sometimes children do (as long as they speak with "inside voices").

After this sort of preliminary work, a researcher would be in a better position to figure out, first, what exactly a particular classroom or school has to teach her or him about a certain phenomenon and, second, how such a study might be organized. For example, if, in a designated bilingual classroom, one hears no language spoken other than English, one might plan a study on the local meaning of being bilingual, but one would not, we suspect, plan a case study of particular children becoming bilingual. Similarly, if children in a classroom complete primarily highly structured tasks (e.g., multiple choice or fill in the blank) and do so under strict sanctions against talking, a researcher would likely find it quite difficult to gather the data necessary for a case study on a childhood culture and its relationship to literacy learning.

Still, initial observations of a site are just that, and therefore they are tentative and usually superficial and one-dimensional. For example, a researcher may make quick jottings about an official reading-group event in a primary grade, but usually when a reading group is meeting, varied other events, differently structured, are simultaneously happening in other areas of the room. Some of these events may be "official," or teacher monitored, and others may be "unofficial," or initiated and monitored by students themselves. Storytelling and teasing events, even singing or quick little dances, can all happen in a time and space within the local physical site but set apart in its components—its purpose, interactional structure, mood, and participation structure—from official time and space. Indeed, even the official reading event may serve varied child and teacher agendas and, moreover, may itself be accompanied or interrupted by varied unofficial events (e.g., teases and jokes done only with a quick facial expression).

All these official and unofficial complexities are hard to see in early visits to potential sites. Researchers, therefore, try to get a sense of the recurrent flow of routine events. The comments of ethnographer Barrie Thorne are relevant here. She spent a great deal of time on school playgrounds trying to understand how gender differences figured into, and were constructed by, children's play. She writes:

> Watching kids day after day, especially on the playground, I was struck by . . . their quick movements and high levels of energy, the rapidity with which they formed and reformed groups and activities. Public schools are unusually crowded environments, which intensifies the sense of chaos; the playgrounds were often thick with moving bodies. At first I felt like a sixteen-millimeter observer trying to grasp the speeded-up motions of a thirty-six-millimeter movie. One of the teachers told me that groups of children reminded her of bumble bees, an apt image of swarms, speech, and constant motion. After I had observed for several months, I saw much more order in the chaos. (Thorne, 1993, p. 14)

Summary

To begin to find order in the chaos—or to disrupt the taken-for-granted familiarity of classrooms where, at first glance, "nothing happens" but "business as usual"—researchers may attune themselves to the rhythms of daily activity. They make maps of figured space and note how time is distributed and how people are arranged in space/time formations.

In language and literacy studies in the interpretive tradition, case study researchers are interested in how teaching and learning happen through social participation. They need an initial lens for getting a sense of the flow of social activity itself, and so they use the culture of research to find etic terms like *event* and *practice* and the analytic language to tentatively describe those activities (Watson-Gegeo, 1988, p. 580). Gradually, one's eyes and ears become accustomed to new sights and sounds, and possibilities for study begin to coalesce, as we illustrate in the two sections to follow.

CASING MRS. KAY'S CLASSROOM (ANNE)

PAM (college student): I think maybe the thing that would turn me off the most is kind of like the actual setting of the school, like where it's at. . . . Driving down you just see these stores without signs and boarded up houses and it's just kind of run down.

The road to a school site, the building itself, the land on which it sits, all become symbols, or texts, to which readers—young teachers-to-be, no less than researchers—bring assumptions and expectations. This is basic to all human interpretation (Hall, 1997). Pam was one of a group of education majors who were having their first field experience in Lyron and Tionna's school. All but one were White; all attended almost exclusively White schools, mainly in suburban settings; and all were grappling with their own opinions about what children would be like in a neighborhood school that wears its economic hard times so openly. Mainly, Pam and her colleagues were worried about behavior, about whether they could control the kids.

Like these young adults, I followed a city map to Lyron and Tionna's school. I too read the road and the building. I was in the process of visiting all district schools that met certain criteria, particularly schools that were high poverty (i.e., the majority of students qualified for the federal lunch program) and "minority majority" (the majority of pupils were children of color). In my view, within such a site I am more likely to learn about cultural resources and, indeed, childhoods themselves that have been undertheorized as contexts for literacy learning (as opposed to school failure). And, if Pam and her colleagues had worries about the children, I had worries about the curricula. Among some of my colleagues, the district had a reputation for rigid textbook-based curricula, heavily regulated by district "pacing" guides.

In order to learn about this site on its own terms, and to figure out what this place might teach me, I had to work to carefully attune myself to its rhythms. In the beginning, this meant sketching maps, asking for official schedules (or copying those that were posted), jotting down the organizational specifics of a breadth of language and literacy activities, and noting how children were arranged in the room—and how they arranged themselves when they had the opportunity to find their own companions in transition periods, free-activity times, and recess.

In this getting-acquainted process, it matters how a researcher (or any other observer) inserts her- or himself into the times and spaces of a site. Listen to another undergraduate, Sharon; she and her colleague Berry had been visiting 2 hours each Wednesday morning in Lyron and Tionna's classroom, taught by Mrs. Kay. In this portion of the group interview that I had with her and five of her colleagues, she has been commenting on her perception of the lack of reading in the room:

SHARON: [The students in Berry's and my class] have, like, a little stack of, you know, books, small books, on their desks. But I've never really seen them read those either. I think what I've seen them using them for is they prop it up between the two kids when there's a test. That's what they use them for. (Laughs) The only time they read is when the teacher reads to them from a book.

BERRY: But that's just our perspective from being there 2 hours in the morning. . . . We're there on the same day at the same time every week.

Sharon had been observing in the classroom for 2½ months when this discussion took place. She spoke with apparent confidence of a lack of reading in Mrs. Kay's room, where books were props to other activities. But, as Berry noted, the window through which he and Sharon gained insight into the classroom was set in a certain slot in the week's time block. And, as Mrs. Kay had told me when I called to set up the first visit, "every day is different." She arranged her own teaching around time slots set by the school so that all classes could share common building spaces set aside for library visits, computer experience, art, and music, as well as recess and public gatherings (i.e., school assemblies) for one occasion or another.

On my own first visit to the school, for an afternoon session, I noted in my informal field notes that the children seemed familiar with, and exceedingly eager to read, the books on their desks in any transition time. When a task was done, a child would ask, "Can we read?" and small hands searched the pile for very particular books. There were shouts of "I got [this or that title]," and a couple of quick walk-runs to another desk cluster to show someone a funny picture or read a funny line.

The children used these books during downtimes or wait times. There were no such times in the Wednesday-morning routine observed by Sharon and Berry, which were whole-class activities on the rug followed by the weekly spelling test, when I, too, saw books transform side-by-side desks into private cubicles.

Similarly, the students thought there might be no child composing in the room (and certainly there were no children's writing products displayed). But there was a writing period at least four times a week during the last 45 minutes of the school day. Mrs. Kay felt that the final event in the writing sequence—the rug-sharing time—provided a "nice note" on which to end the school day.

There is a need, then, to attend deliberately to time and space in getting to know any site. Even if one planned, for example, to do a case study of the life of a reading group that group's structure and its evident forms of teacher and child agency would be meaningful to all concerned in part because of the time and space it occupied in the landscape of the school. Moreover, there is a need to articulate and bracket one's evaluative urges. Varied observers noting exactly the same behaviors might easily draw strikingly different evaluations of those behaviors. In the end, the qualitative case study researchers want to interpret those behaviors by understanding their varied meanings in the experiential world they are hoping to enter.

Consider, one last time, the comments of the young teachers-to-be at Mrs. Kay's school.

SHARON: [The class] was doing this exercise where they correct grammar. And one child said something and it was wrong. . . . And another student yelled out, "Ah-ha he gotted it wrong." Well, you know, there's the pot calling the kettle black.

BERRY: [The children get] a lot less Standard English than when we went to school. We were taught Standard English grammar. . . . [I]n the morning they'll do an activity where they'll have sentences on an easel and they'll go through and correct them for grammar and punctuation and that kind of thing. . . . So there's a little bit of teaching of Standard English there, but when that's done, there's, you know, if the students say something incorrectly or [in] a nonstandard form of English, nothing is said about it.

For the students, the lack of "correction" suggested a lack of "teaching" Standard English, which seemed to be their understanding of how they had learned Standard English.

Unlike the students, I was not visiting the school as part of an effort to learn to teach. I was trying to locate a site that would contribute to the understanding of children and literacy. Moreover, I had a sociolinguistic frame that the students had not had the opportunity to experience. I saw what the students saw; my observations, however, led not to evaluations but to questions. This is the way of the researcher.

So, in my early visits to this site, I jotted down the kinds of literacy events that occurred. In so doing, I noted the substantial role for editing, including editing for usage. In the afternoon, when Mrs. Kay modeled her own writing, she engaged in such editing of her text; during free writing time, she helped individual children edit their own entries; and, as the students reported, during the morning Mrs. Kay asked children to find errors, including those of usage, in provided sentences. At the beginning of a writing period, Mrs. Kay might say that the children could "talk about" whatever they wanted in their writing. To cue children to consider usage errors, Mrs. Kay said, "Does that sound right?" Some of the corrections involved developmental errors evident in children's learning of varied varieties of English (e.g., "gotted"), but many involved usage patterns that were grammatical in nonstandard Englishes (e.g., "they was"). Such varieties seemed to be spoken by almost all the children in the room and thus must have "sounded right," or so it seemed to me.

At the same time, as the students noted, there seemed to be no correction throughout most "talk" events in this classroom, including the many personal storytelling events. These occurred throughout the day in both formal lessons and informal interactions. Indeed, Mrs. Kay conceived of the afternoon writing time as children's opportunity to "tell the story of their lives."

I started to wonder about the kind of language ideology present in the district curricula, objectives, and tests. And I wondered, too, what these young children were making of written expression. What did they have to "say" during and about official writing? What kind of language resources did they draw on? How did they construct and narrate their own childhoods on and off paper as they participated in official writing events? Were there unofficial writing events? As questions began to formulate, so too did a more formal study design. I decided to stay on in Mrs. Kay's lively, talk-filled classroom, with its interesting contradictions about children having their "say."

CASING MS. YUNG'S CLASSROOM (CELIA)

The first official researcher on the case in Donna Yung-Chan's room was Susan Stires, a staff developer at the pre-kindergarten (pre-k) through Grade 5 school who was on the lookout for an early childhood classroom that was also lively and talk filled. In Donna and Susan's school, some of the talk was in languages other than English, a characteristic that appealed to all three of us and that we have focused on in our collaborative writing (Genishi, et al., 2001; Genishi, et al., 2000). Nonetheless, Donna was the lead teacher in a "general education" pre-k that was not categorized as a bilingual or English-as-a-second-language setting. What follows in this section is invisible in our articles, as I reflect on casing a place that my coresearchers already knew and that we all suspected would soon become our shared research site.

Our site is in New York City, which most people would find completely unlike a midsized city in the Midwest. But, like Anne, I was seeking a minority-majority school at a time when curricula were narrowing under the pressure of local mandates to improve achievement test scores in reading and math, with the emphasis on reading. I work in a college of education in which the diverse student population, including the 25 to 30% who are of color, have little experience with schools like Donna and Susan's. At their school, the vast majority of children qualify for the federal lunch program; thus the children are similar to one another in economic background yet are diverse culturally and linguistically. Within this milieu I was eager to find a place where the language and literacy curriculum for young children was not narrow, but open to talk in English and other languages. I felt optimistic that Donna's pre-k classroom had much to teach us about teaching and learning, particularly English-language learning. One of our research goals was to create interpretive descriptions that would introduce readers, like my college students, to diverse learners and teachers in a particular sociopolitical, cultural, and educational setting—a setting to which I also needed an introduction.

Fortunately Susan was in "guide mode," and, since we lived in the same neighborhood uptown, we arranged to meet for the trip downtown. Feeling a bit like Madlenka no longer on her block, I checked a subway map to orient myself the night before the first visit. The trip involved one subway transfer, and Susan gave advice and commentary about which subway to take and which landmarks to walk by and through on the 10-minute walk to the school. On subsequent trips on my own, I emerged alone from one of the subway stations near Chinatown and tried to remember Susan's directions because there were multiple routes I could take. I would make mental and written notes of the landmarks—City Hall, the Brooklyn Bridge, large apartment buildings, neighborhood shops with signs written in Chinese—all material for curricula for young English-language learners, from my point of view.

Indeed neighborhood landmarks did become part of the spoken, drawn, written, and otherwise constructed curriculum in Donna's room. Because she and Susan already knew the classroom well before the formal study began, I was the one who needed to spend some time casing the pre-k site, observing how the people who were routinely there organized themselves in the time and space of their school days. I usually visited in the mornings before the children's lunch and rest times, influenced by my schedule (I taught my own classes in the afternoon) and by the local adage that "everything happens in the morning" in public schools. As it turned out, I saw that things happened in the afternoon, too, since the day ended at about 3:00 P.M. The class schedule was posted at the children's eye level, and, though I didn't visit often, there were times when a field trip to the public library or a rehearsal for the end-of-year music fest provided added texture for the rhythm of life in this school.

In retrospect, it seems that I looked for ways of describing this rhythm by relying on the organizational units of my past. The pre-k classrooms I knew were full of talk and movement, and I tended to orient myself by focusing on curricular or in-dividual units that "chunked" the talk and movement, such as activities that lasted for a certain period of time or a child to observe for a set time. In Ms. Yung's room, the morning circle time, called in other rooms "morning meeting," included a fo-cus on the calendar and the day's weather. (From this point on, I will call Donna "Ms. Yung" to refer to her in-classroom name and identity.) As a newcomer, I was taken by the amount of talk (in both Cantonese and English, but mostly in English) and the amount of repetition within this chunk of time.

The predictability of routines that initiated each day (the first was breakfast) was a striking contrast to what children did during "activity" time, what some preschool teachers might call "choice time." Children chose their activity—the choosing process was called "planning" on the daily schedule—and it ranged from playing in the housekeeping area to using math manipulatives to doing art to using computers. I noted the time periodically as I chose individual children as my obser-vational "unit." For example, I wrote quick notes about how Ashley stood at the easel and created a blend of greens and reds, holding a paintbrush in each hand—she was not a left- or right-handed but a two-handed artist. She painted without talking until Ms. Yung asked her if she was finished with her painting and wanted to hang it up; Ashley said yes.

I also noted that some children came to the classroom after circle time ended, often with a parent or grandparent who talked with Ms. Yung—especially if she or he spoke only Cantonese—or with the assistant teacher, Ms. Cipriano, to explain the lateness. The posted schedule was not so rigid that these late entrances caused disruption. In fact, while I observed, there were various interruptions as other teachers took children out for special services, so days were punctuated by intrusions that appeared to be routine.

Lunchtime seemed to be a welcome intrusion. (Pre-k children's meals are delivered to their rooms in public schools that are supported by the federal lunch program.) Moreover, washing up before and after lunch was a routine popular with some children and not with others. This classroom was located near the children's bathrooms, as well as the teachers'. Thus, walks down the hall were short and, when I was observing, uneventful. Lunch was followed by rest time, which was followed by another activity time and afternoon circle time. In sum, these observations reflected what I saw in several visits, and I inferred that the daily schedule was moderately flexible. Even breakfast and lunchtimes were not rigid; the class's turn on the playground, however, was fixed.

As in the world outside of schools, time and space in Ms. Yung's room were intimately linked. Her room, on the second floor of a 100-year-old building, was square and, like most public school classrooms, not spacious. A map would reveal three open spaces, one for dramatic play, one for block construction, and a third for circle time. When people were present, though, the block and circle areas became multipurpose zones. Children might lie on the rug in the block or circle area to share books, for example. Space, then, was also tied to activities.

Bookcases, containing—in addition to books—such things as manipulatives, puzzles, and art materials, separated the areas. Two of these were filled with sets of tables, one set for the use of manipulatives and the other for art activities and writing. The first set of tables doubled as the breakfast, lunch, and snack area. Close to the circle area was the computer, which Ms. Yung used to review the weather each morning and which children could choose as an activity. As in most spaces for young children, objects and materials were not used or stored only on tables, in bookcases, or on the floor. One wall was lined with a narrow closet for adults' coats and belongings and the children's storage areas—their cubbies—personalized with their names and a symbol, like a car or a butterfly, which was also theirs. Another wall was hidden by the pile of children's mats for rest time. Other walls displayed children's work, which also covered some of the extensive window space or was suspended from clothesline-like cords.

Ms. Yung's classroom was clearly a "people place"—people coming in and out; people visiting (like me) or carrying out a student field placement; people living their daily lives there, choosing and doing things; and, much of the time, people doing things through talk. There were many adults and children present with knowledge to share with researchers. Further, I felt confident that this was a social unit where everyone was encouraged to focus on language and early literacy learning at the same time that they could take language for granted. That is, it was a constant resource, which was discouraged only when children got very loud or disrupted others' talk or work. Adults seemed to accept the language forms that children used, whether they were in English, Cantonese, or dialects like Fujianese. Of course, questions came to mind about how to learn from people in Ms. Yung's room: Since we might begin data collection in the spring, how much of children's language use would be retrievable or remembered by either Ms. Yung or Susan? How could we answer general questions about English-language learning? The school was known for its emphasis on literacy; to what extent would Ms. Yung's integrated curriculum remain so as the end of the year approached (and pre-k teachers are urged to think about whether their children are ready for kindergarten)? To what extent would patterns of language use change?

Summary

The "casing phase" offers a researcher the luxury of looking through her own lens, which is open to her interests, predilections, and particular skills. At the same time she works to keep the lens clear enough so the questions she begins to formulate are relevant to the site; that is, they grow out of what she sees and experiences. What I saw during my early visits to Ms. Yung and Susan's school was global as I looked broadly at the children and the curriculum. Questions about language and literacy learning were embedded within my holistic looks. In terms of an evolving case study, I expected Ms. Yung and Susan, positioned in other locations in the same space, to enhance my vision through their regular presence and greater knowledge of the children, curriculum, and school.

DOCUMENTING THE RESEARCH JOURNEY

As our early visits to Mrs. Kay's and Ms. Yung's classrooms show, initiating a qualitative case study is akin to starting a journey without a clearly marked route. Indeed, one's first task is to get a sense of the map of the terrain, that is, of the configuration and distribution of time, space, and people, and of the dynamics of social activity. Unlike in traditional experiments, the study design is not set from the beginning. The design will come from strategic decision-making, as one's knowledge of a site and one's particular inquiry interests inform each other.

Still, from the very beginning, researchers write; they turn "lived experience into bit[s] of written text" (Emerson, et al., 1995, p. vii). Quite quickly, the unfamiliar aspects of a new site can become familiar and taken for granted. Initial responses and curiosities can be forgotten, as can potential avenues for inquiry. Moreover, schedules, maps, lists, documents—all may become odd piles of yellowing paper if they are not filed and recorded.

In the beginning of the study, a project notebook can prove useful. The notebook, with consecutively numbered pages, can be a place to record even the very first contacts with a site—initial phone calls, names and numbers of contacts, any circulating gossip about the site, initial observations and reflections, and, later, formal field notes (discussed in Chapter 4). The notebook might begin with an evolving Table of Contents, as in Figure 2.1, to help one recall exactly where and when one noted what. At the same time, file folders for curricular documents, newspaper clippings, and school brochures might be organized before those artifacts retreat into corners of offices, the depths of tote bags, the odd pocket of this or that jacket.

Figure 2.1. Project Notebook: Initial Contacts

TABLE OF CONTENTS

Important Numbers:

      Donna—555–222–1111
      Susan—555–222–3333
      School—555–222–1234 (8 Henry St)

Chronology of Contacts and Visits:

      May 10, 1997—talked with Susan about possibility of research collaboration in a pre-k classroom
      June, 1997—I met Donna; Susan talked with Donna and their principal about the project. They want to participate.
      July, 1997—proposal draft goes back and forth
      Aug 1, 1997—proposal sent to Spencer Foundation
      Jan 6, 1998—receive letter of approval; proposal sent to NYC Board of Ed
      Jan, 1998—receive approval from Board of Ed; Susan starts preliminary field notes
      Feb 26, 1998—call Donna to arrange my visit
      Mar 2, 1998—first visit to Donna's school with Susan

Scratch Notes:

      Took #2 subway—try to be in one of the first cars so can get out where I should. Various ways of approaching school; went by City Hall and Municipal Bldg. School in lovely old bldg. Met principal; had quick tour. Open and welcoming feeling about school; lovely child-made quilt on wall of stairwell to celebrate 100th anniversary of school.

After Classroom Observation:

Entry #	Date	Pages	Activities	Comment
1	3/2/98	1–4	breakfast thru activity time	Took few notes; tried to get sense of people, schedule, "lay of land" (map)

Many scholars have stressed the centrality of writing to a qualitative enterprise: The researcher *"writes it down"* (Geertz, 1973, p. 19 [emphasis in original]; also, Clifford & Marcus, 1986; Feld & Basso, 1996; Sanjek, 1990). We add that the researcher also numbers, paginates, and files.

SUMMARY: "THE WORLD AROUND HERE"

We began this chapter with Geertz's observation that nobody exists outside time and space; everybody lives in some particular and confined "world around here" (1996, p. 262). In this chapter, we have discussed the process of casing somebody else's joint—somebody else's world. This casing involved

- attending to the configuration and distribution of space, time, and people;
- using sociolinguistic concepts to note the social dynamics of classroom events; and
- recording and filing information gathered.

The casing process is well summarized by Bogdan and Biklen:

> [R]esearchers scout for possible places and people that might be the subject or the source of data, find the location they think they want to study, and then cast a wide net trying to judge the feasibility of the site or data source for their purposes. They look for clues on how they might proceed and what might be feasible to do. (2003, p. 54)

And then the work begins to take focus, as time and place, people and activities, come more clearly into view. Questions begin to formulate; possible ways to anchor the study in some bounded social unit—some case—begin to be considered. It is time for directed data collection to begin. But before that can happen, there are some strategic decisions to be made. In the following chapter, we highlight key decisions to be made in case study design.

CHAPTER 3

Getting on the Case: Case Study Design

And so
he said,
"Do this:
go get to know
one thing
as well
as you can.

It should be
something
small. . . ."
(Baylor & Parnall, 1978, n. p.) [1]

T his is the sage advice of the character called "an old man" in Byrd Baylor and Peter Parnall's *The Other Way to Listen*. When his young companion asks him how we learn to hear the subtle sounds of nature, the old man advises getting "to know one thing as well as you can." In other words, choose something small and observe it intentionally and closely over time. Similarly, in the world of research we seek to know something as well as we can, and we look for guidance, since we usually feel that there are too many interesting things to know and way too little time to observe them all closely.

In this chapter we try to segment the time it takes to know something well, realizing that naming a segment (for example, "phase 1") is useful but arbitrary. In reality the different phases of a study often blend one into the next, and so beginning to get to know one thing well—"casing the joint"—may be hard to separate from "getting on the case." Here we focus on what happens once the joint is cased: identifying the case, locating ourselves as researchers within it, then making decisions about how we will carry out the study—that is, designing the study.

IDENTIFYING THE CASE: FOREGROUND AND BACKGROUND

In the academic world, where researchers are often required to write a proposal about the study they plan to carry out, potential joints to be studied are sometimes cased during an exploratory or pilot phase. The fervent hope is that this phase, the start of getting to know something well will help to place boundaries around spaces and times of interest, so that we can identify "the case." Heeding the advice of an old man, we can decide that a young girl and her loose tooth constitute "something small," both interesting and manageable. Of course every "something" exists within a context, which defines the case and teaches us about the "something small." Thus in the preceding chapter we decided that a city block might set the spatial boundary of a case of intergenerational learning, an abstract phenomenon made concrete by people like Madlenka and her neighbors, what we called in Chapter 1 a small, naturalistic social unit. In the world around us—the educational world—we might say that naturalistic social units are easy to locate, since schools and classrooms and individual children and teachers within them appear at first to present themselves as cases waiting to be studied. But as we suggested in Chapter 2, it is not always clear what a child, teacher, room, or school is "a case of."

Understanding that Madlenka's block is potentially a case of intergenerational learning or that Mrs. Kay's room is a case of children's "having their say" depends on knowing both background and foreground. That is, each case becomes an object of study—the foreground—against a particular background or problem that animates the researcher to see the boundaries of the case. The problem animating a study of Madlenka's block could be the lack of documentation of funds of knowledge (Moll, 1992) that young children acquire with people of another generation in densely populated areas of industrialized countries. Underlying this problem might be a belief (perhaps a stereotype) that a child in a large city leads an insular life untouched by neighbors and especially by neighbors unlike her parents or other family members. Such a problematic background gives the study substance and a reason for being—in short, its visible point. Over time we formulate specific questions about happenings on Madlenka's block and what they might mean.

The problem underlying the study with Donna Yung-Chan and Susan Stires was a growing one that could be summed up by the tongue-tying phrase "the over-academicization of early childhood education." This pithy quote from the *New York Times* captured the growing pressure to transform early schooling into dens of reading, writing, and 'rithmetic:

> No more fun and games: As children across the nation head back to school this fall, many are encountering a harsher atmosphere in which states set specific academic standards and impose real penalties on those who do not meet them. (Lewin, 1999, p. A-1)

In 2004 the political realities of schooling continue to provide the background for studies of educational spaces, especially with respect to language and literacy learning.

Indeed, in Mrs. Kay's classroom the problem underlying the case was also related to the political realities of schooling, set against the sociocultural ones of children's daily lives. In her classroom, as in many others nationwide, there was increased emphasis on "the basics," as traditionally interpreted (e.g., on writing mechanics and grammatical usage). The language ideology governing those basics presupposed a singular way of speaking and writing correctly, whatever the situation, whoever the communicators. However, listening to Mrs. Kay's children revealed the cultural and linguistic diversity commonplace in urbanized areas all over the country. In such a situation, what do "the basics" mean to the teaching and learning challenges of Mrs. Kay and her children, and, more broadly, what do they reveal about the imagined society for which children are to be prepared?

Formulating Questions to Shape the Study

Just as identifying the case and the problem and putting boundaries around the times, spaces, and people of interest provide a framework for case study research, formulating a research question or questions gives shape to the overall design of the study. Indeed, we have heard and read many times that decisions about design always depend on our questions. At the same time we have heard and read that the questions should not constrain us. For example, Bogdan and Biklen (2003, p. 49) write plainly, "Our advice is to hang loose"—or loose enough so that questions can change in response to the researcher's experiences or observations. Thus if it turns out that Madlenka seeks out her neighbors only when there is a major event to announce, the researcher may decide to look for a new site or, if her relationship with Madlenka shows promise, she will stay in the world around Madlenka but seek a new phenomenon to study there. If additional casing reveals that peer learning is significant in her world, the overall question might become, How do young children learn from one another in a particular out-of-school world? One thing that we have learned about formulating questions is that, like everything else in case study research, it happens over time—so anticipate articulating a question or questions and then the probability of revising.

Designing the Study

In the academic worlds around us, the challenge to researchers, especially beginning researchers, is to hang loose, but not too loose. Even citing the appealing advice of Bogdan and Biklen (2003) may not deter advisors from asking their students, "So what exactly are you studying here?" And experienced researchers in search of funding hear similar queries.

Data Collection in Ms. Yung's Classroom (Celia)

In my study with Donna Yung-Chan and Susan Stires, for which we sought and obtained a small grant, we created an overall design for our study, describing Donna's classroom and our general plan for data collection. The majority of the children in this classroom came from homes where Cantonese was the primary and sometimes the only language spoken, and often two or three children came from homes where Spanish was spoken. During the year of the study, there were no Spanish speakers, but there were two biracial children whose primary language was English. Donna was particularly concerned with her English-language learners' vocabulary development in relation to the common objects and events in their worlds. Thus her general research question was, How do children expand their vocabularies through language experiences?

This was our plan for data collection:

> Susan will work in the classroom 3 days a week for approximately an hour per day during the period of the integrated language study. She will work directly with the children on a variety of projects depending on the classroom activities, but particularly on language experience in order to maximize opportunities to record language. She will take field notes and record language using audio- and videotaping. Videotaping will be done no more than once a week, to avoid collecting unmanageable amounts of data. Susan will meet with Donna Yung-Chan after each session to discuss what she has observed and receive updates from Donna about events when she was not in the classroom. All three researchers will read and discuss the implications of oral language studies conducted in other classrooms or summaries of such research. (Yung-Chan, Stires, & Genishi, 1997, p. 4)

The decisions embedded in this brief plan grew out of conversations about what would be least disruptive to the everyday workings of Donna's class. The number of times Susan was to observe also depended on her work schedule as a staff developer. She wedged her research visits in between staff development sessions, guessing that there would be weeks when three visits would not be possible or when Donna would not be free to meet with her to debrief or elaborate. Once the study began, this overall design served as a road map, one that was much less detailed and more flexible than the service station variety.

If, however, an advisor, school administrator, or funder required a more detailed design, a time line like that in Figure 3.1 might be created, with the overall goal of answering the question, "How do children expand their vocabularies through language experiences?" As the study unfolds, the question could change in response to the ways in which Donna's children are actually using and learning language. Thus we could later add a column to the table to include additional research questions or shifting areas of focus; for example, individual children

Figure 3.1. Proposing the Case in Ms. Yung's Room: Timeline

Dates	Observer and Method	Focus
Jan.–Feb. '98	Susan—field notes	Classroom; all activities
Mar. '98	Celia—field notes, audiotaping	A.M. activities; individual children
Mar.–May '98	Susan—field notes, audiotaping, video-taping	Alternating A.M. and P.M. activities; individual children
May–June '98	Susan, Celia—field notes, videotaping	Selected A.M.'s and P.M.'s; children needing addtional observations

might no longer be the observed "unit" if a focus on activities provided more information. Shifts in design like these are elaborated upon in Chapter 4.

Data Collection in Mrs. Kay's Classroom (Anne)

In my study in Mrs. Kay's classroom, data collection also took place according to a set but flexible plan. The plan was informed by the project's two overarching sets of questions. The first set was about the official curriculum. I wondered, What are the basics of teaching children to write, as defined in this school site? What kinds of district policies and documents inform these basics? What social and language values (that is, what ideologies) undergird these basics?

To answer these questions, I needed to observe most intensely the writing curriculum. And, using a sociocultural frame, I assumed that that curriculum would play itself out in varied kinds of writing practices (e.g., teacher modeling, editing conferences, journal-writing times), and that those practices would involve certain social relationships between and among teacher and children, certain materials, and certain ways of talking about the use of written symbols themselves. I was especially eager to document the interactive guidance that Mrs. Kay offered children, especially that couched in evaluative language—about what's "good" or "needs to be made better" in the children's efforts.

I had spent the first month of the project casing the joint, as it were, and I knew that most language activities involving writing were in the afternoon. And so I planned to observe 5 hours a week, usually spread over 2 days (but sometimes 3 or 4 if my semester classes were not in session or the children had been out of school for several days). I also planned to audiotape whenever I observed, along with taking scratch notes (rough notes to be typed up as field notes). I knew that I would not be able to transcribe all the audiotapes, without giving up eating and sleeping routines, but I also knew that, during analysis, I could transcribe "key events," that is, events that seemed particularly informative relative to my questions. Finally, I also planned to borrow curricular guidelines and texts from Mrs. Kay and to print out relevant district, state, and federal documents from the Internet.

The second set of questions was the one I was most excited about. I wanted to understand, How do the children interpret the "basic" lessons and activities? What experiential, linguistic, and textual resources do they draw on as they participate in the "basics"? I was especially interested in the children's evaluative language about written symbols. What did they consider "problems" in their own writing? What decisions did they make in an effort to solve perceived problems?

An interest in children's resources as children, as members of the cultures of childhood, had two important implications for my plan. First, I could not observe only in official events, since children's resources—their experiences with popular texts, like video games and cartoons; their repertoire of ways of speaking; their ways of managing relationships with one another—may be most visible when children are outside an assigned official task. So I planned to begin my observations during lunchtime recess, then observe reading group time, a free choice period or another quick recess (weather permitting), a social studies or science lesson, and, then, finally, the events of "writing time."

Second, observing writing is a very fine-grained affair. I have to hear the children's talk; see the process by which the drawing or writing takes shape on the page and how it is interwoven with talk to self, to teacher, to peers; and pay attention to if and how the children's texts are coordinated with those of others. I find it easiest to have one child be the anchor point during writing tasks, so that I can discipline my attention.

For this reason, I needed to make decisions about internal sampling, that is, about sampling from all the potential activities and participants who could be observed or learned from within the boundaries of the case (in my project, within the classroom). For example, sometimes there are certain people, or key informants, whom researchers talk with in order to get varied angles on what's going on relative to some phenomenon. In my project, I chose three focal children (children whom I would regularly observe in fine-grained ways). In choosing the focal children, I was guided by the need to gain a comprehensive description of child resources for participating in lessons on the basics. Because gender and ethnic culture figure into childhood cultures and resources, I chose children who varied in these ways. I did not intend to generalize from, say, Tionna to all African American children or from Ezekial to all Mexican American kids. But I did intend that their resources, including any particular to their heritages, would figure into my project. Because all the children were low income, I did not consider social class in choosing focal children. However, I did choose children who were comfortable with one another but who also interacted with different configurations of peers. In this way, observing these three focal children would bring into my viewing frame most children in the room.

Our research plans have stressed how we organized our efforts to gain information, or data, which would help us answer our initial questions about language and literacy. But we have not yet considered how we organized our selves, so to speak, for entering into our cases. This is the design issue to which we now turn.

LOCATING OURSELVES WITHIN THE CASE: WHO ARE WE?

As we suggested earlier, planning and doing research is all about making decisions. In this section we raise and complicate the question of deciding who we are within the case. Who the researcher is or becomes in an educational setting is outlined in the study's design, for the role she takes on influences what kinds of data she can gather. Returning again to the

world around Madlenka, however, we see how the researcher's role is merely "outlined" in the overall design. Until the
researcher engages regularly with that world, she won't know
the nature and boundaries of her role. And although she noted
that Madlenka was a "potentially good informant," opportunities to tap that potential will depend on concrete matters of
scheduling and on the nature of relationships supported by
the scheduling and the temperaments of participants and researcher. Further, when the main participant is a young child,
the researcher needs to consider how adults in Madlenka's
world will view the researcher and her activities.

Taking on a Researcher's Role

Multiple questions occur to a researcher before she officially gets on the case: How will I dress? Where will I sit? How
much should I talk with people in the classroom, and in what
kind of language? Will the children expect me to act like an
assistant teacher now that I'll be visiting more often? And if
I decide to assist, how will I work in the extra visits when I'll
help particular children?

Questions like these reflect the range of roles that a researcher may take on while on the case, or put another way,
the varied ways in which she might position herself or be positioned as a researcher. The researcher routinely observes the
classroom participants, and, of course, they have opportunities
to observe her. Her research questions influence the extent to
which she remains outside the events to be studied or gains
access to become an insider. Thus the decision about what to
wear isn't a trivial one; adults and children in the classroom
will not expect someone in an elegant suit to sit on a child-
sized chair or the floor to talk with children (though she or
he might do that). In contrast a woman in pants and a casual sweater similar to the teacher's might be approached by a
child for help with a classroom task. One outfit sends a message from an outsider, whereas the other conveys a different
message by means of its ordinariness.

Looking ordinary may soon lead to going unnoticed so that adults and children either accept the researcher as another helpful person, like most adults in the room, or as an unobtrusive visitor. And participants in every research site might define one differently. Graue (Graue & Walsh, 1998, Chapter 5), for instance, was eager to take on the role of instructional aide, but found that within the same study school staff viewed her in that role in only one of the three sites she was studying. The studies that we have individually been part of have led to taking on less participatory, but still complex, roles.

Negotiating a Role in Mrs. Kay's Room (Anne)

In my project in Mrs. Kay's room, I planned to adopt a role as an unhelpful but attentive adult friend of children. I aimed for such a role because I wanted to gain access to aspects of children's worlds that may be hidden from authority figures (e.g., their nonacademic talk when "working"). I began negotiating this role with Mrs. Kay even before I formally decided to do the project in her room. I was comfortable with Mrs. Kay because I felt no urge to evaluate or second-guess her teaching (as opposed to her mandated curricular guidelines). She interacted with the children in ways I judged responsive and respectful; at the same time, she worked hard to meet district expectations. But I needed to be sure that Mrs. Kay would be comfortable with me.

I explicitly told Mrs. Kay that I would not be able to either instruct or discipline the children, but that I would be very happy to help in other ways (e.g., helping distribute supplies, tracking down materials, and talking with her about my observations of children). Mrs. Kay was agreeable to this, mainly because she was interested in my approach. She, in fact, knew a great deal about the children's nonacademic lives, shared this information readily, and even gave me a tour of the neighborhood, pointing out where each child lived.

In negotiating my role with the children, I planned to rely, in part, on time—that is, on becoming a regular, nonjudgmental, attentive classroom participant. To some extent, I intended to adopt the "reactive" stance so well articulated by Corsaro (2003): I would not ask children their names and would mainly speak when spoken to. However, unlike Corsaro, who participated with younger children in nonacademic tasks (e.g., sand play), I did not intend to join in activities with the children. That would seem quite phony. (As a child once said to me, "You should know this stuff by now.") Rather, as is my usual approach, I planned to explain to the children that I was very interested in what it was like to be a little kid at school and that my job would be to write down what they did. I would be "very, very busy" writing down what they did, and so I would not be able to help them do their work.

Being "busy" is understood by children. However, in practice, I did not always maintain this stance. For example, if a child was just sure I would want to interrupt my work to hear a story she or he had just written, I tended to do so, relying on my tape recorder to help fill in my observational gaps. I tied shoes, struggled with zippers, and retrieved tissues for dripping noses, even as I listened to unsanctioned talk, peered over a child's shoulder at a clandestine love note, and silently witnessed snacking from an out-of-place bag of chips.

In negotiating researcher roles, certainly age, gender, race, and language all matter. In negotiating roles with young children in mid-Michigan, just as in my previous location (the Bay Area), I have been particularly conscious of race, because the children are. For example, close friendships tend to be racially homogeneous, especially among girls. As a White woman, I planned to rely here too on the regularity of my presence over time, as well as on the good graces of certain focal children. In Mrs. Kay's room, for example, Tionna was comfortable with my sitting beside her. From the beginning, she paid me no particular mind, but as time when on we chatted on occasion about this or that. I knew that if Tionna was comfortable with me, her friends would probably become comfortable with me, too, and this is what happened.

Finally, in negotiating roles with children, I knew that I needed to learn as much as possible about the neighborhood and, also, the assorted places and media sources referenced by the children. Knowing the radio station the children listened to, the cartoons they enjoyed, and the stores their families frequented would help me carry on conversations with the children during lunchtime or while walking out to the playground, and it would gradually allow me to become somebody other than a teacher, a quiet, passive, but accepted adult friend.

Varied Roles in Ms. Yung's Room (Celia)

In a collaborative study, researchers need some time to sort out what their roles will be. Following Susan and Donna—who was becoming a researcher in her own room—as the third researcher on the case, I was the latecomer. Pre-k classroom routines were already well established, and many children were fluent English-language learners by February, when the study officially began. Yet there were research decisions to be made related to the focus of our study and our respective roles in the collaboration. As we pointed out earlier, how one inserts oneself into the times and spaces of a site does matter; and the *how* becomes more complex when there is a team of researchers.

In our developing study, familiarity with the community and setting and with the relationships of power made a difference. Donna and Susan were already familiar with the community around the school, the school, and the classroom itself—its time allotments, spatial arrangements, and human relationships. I came with a naive eye—at least naive to this particular room and group of participants—and I had no official role to play in the school. Thus if we wanted an insider's view, which would provide a context and history for what we all observed, Susan might be the ideal frequent observer. As the primary insider, Donna would be busy most of the time in her teaching role, and I was not yet familiar with the site.

So as the study began, we outlined each researcher's role in ways respectful of classroom schedules and participants' other roles. To the extent possible Susan would separate her staff-developer role from her researcher role; Donna would reserve some time to be an observer-researcher, rather than a participant; and I would be an occasional observer, a relative stranger, who might ask clarifying questions or see the classroom and the people in it from a distinct angle.

We researchers also saw each other in particular ways. Despite our comfort with one another, my role as a college professor (at that time I was Susan's "teacher," too) and lack of official on-site job created a power differential that made my presence more intrusive than Susan's. However, Donna and Susan were more powerful from my and the children's vantage point: They were less likely to ask me for help or information. Also important pragmatically was the popularity of Donna's room with adult visitors and observers from other colleges. The classroom was not spacious, and my regular presence would make it less so.

As the study developed, our respective roles were not always easily bracketed, and being an "objective" observer with tamped-down evaluative urges was at times difficult for me and especially for Susan, whose school job was to instill positive changes in Donna's room.

Beyond Behavior: Addressing Who We Are

Long-standing epistemological questions about how we come to know a phenomenon have reemerged with force recently with the federal government's emphasis on "scientific evidence" in educational research (Cochran-Smith, 2004). In the traditional view of science, researchers come to know the *truth* about a phenomenon, such as how children acquire a language or learn to read, through specified methods in which variables—such as learners and their degree of learning—are controlled and accurately measured. In this view, accurate ways of measuring make the collected evidence scientific. In the grand schemes of research, though, this is one among a growing number of views of research. So in this section we include possible responses from other qualitative researchers and ourselves to the question of who we are as researchers when we engage in case study research. As you have already seen through our examples, our researching selves are essential within the case. Thus we counter "a tendency to view the self of the social science observer as a potential contaminant, something to be separated out, neutralized, minimized, standardized, and controlled" (Weis & Fine, 2000, p. 34). Like curly hair on a damp day, the people who interest us, doing what they usually do, are not easily standardized or controlled, and neither are our researchers' ways of looking, listening, and interpreting.

We do, of course, support systematic ways of doing research that are carefully detailed, whether we are documenting what participants are doing or reflecting on our own research practices. So our data include notes about ourselves.

In two contrasting studies, I (Celia) wrote comments to myself about my reactions to the classroom setting I was observing. In a bilingual kindergarten (Spanish and English) I wrote:

> This is not the way I'd teach kindergartners, but the kids in this room don't seem at all unhappy. Ms.——— wants me to talk to her about what she could be doing better, but I'm not sure I know since her goals for the class are not what mine would be. Also I'm not really sure that she wants to know how to change her teaching.

In the end I positioned myself as an observer who shared findings with the teacher and the principal of the school. She in turn added my observations to her already positive evaluations of Ms.———'s teaching. She also viewed the findings as support for the particular bilingual program she had initiated. Thus my role became that of a short-term documenter.

In contrast, while getting to know Ms. Yung's room, I knew from conversations with Donna and Susan that the practices here were generally compatible with my philosophy of working with young children. Since my role was collaborative and complementary, I sometimes thought about ways in which I differed from my coresearchers. For example:

> You can tell that I was the one videotaping when you look at the tape from last week. It's hard for me not to focus the camera on individual children, rather than larger units, like areas of the room with groups of children— though I did that once I realized that I wasn't recording the bigger picture. I should think about how my way of collecting data fits in with Susan's.

What is clear here is that my eyes, when taking in Donna's class, are not neutral. Rather, I look through figurative and literal lenses guided by preferences and theories that continually position me as a distinctive, researching self.

Complicating Our Roles and Identities

When we write of our researching roles, we can focus on how they unfold as we live through the study; that is, we describe our behaviors at the research site in terms of our actions and our developing relationships with the participants. As already suggested, we might also reflect on particular aspects of our selves that influence the lenses we look through. That is, every person has a biography that precedes her existence as a researcher, incorporating characteristics like race, class, gender, and ability. So, for example, Celia has overlapping identities as a Japanese American, former Japanese speaker, early childhood educator, former Spanish teacher, feminist, political liberal from a working-class family, and so on. Anne names certain aspects of herself in ways similar to those of Celia—for example, her non-middle-class roots, her political bent, her professional identification as a teacher of young children. Others she names differently—for example, her race and her religious upbringing. We recognize that who we are outside our identities as university researchers influences the kinds of questions we ask and the kinds of collaborators and participants we select for our studies. Who we each are also figures into how we collect, analyze, and interpret data, topics we elaborate upon in the following two chapters.

How, then, do we work like ethnographers—who write down or document what they observe or experience—supposedly maintaining some social distance from participants? Doing this requires us to reflect on which lenses we look through and what kinds of relationships suit who we are within a particular research context. Thus we may behave like rather shy friends who speak seldom and write often. Maintaining a balance between distance and intimacy is a continual challenge, as we researchers are a certain kind of guest in a shared space, and some hosts are eager to be conversationalists. So it might be useful to remember Geertz's (1973, p. 13) words, "We are not, or at least I am not, seeking either to become natives . . . or to mimic them. Only romantics or spies would seem to find point in that."

In sum, as researchers on our respective cases we acknowledge that the way we come to know one thing well is a complicated, humanistic process. Each researcher, a person with overlapping identities, plays multiple roles as curious and friendly newcomer and scout, observer, perhaps participant, note taker, audio- or videographer, and so on as we learn from informants or participants in the small part of the world we now call a case. We are the primary instruments of research, relying on the curiosity, friendliness, and acceptance of those who regularly inhabit that world.

Summary

In this chapter we have addressed practical aspects of getting on the case, and we initially had the company of "an old man," who told us of the importance of getting to know one thing well, and of Madlenka, our now-familiar young city dweller. Together their literary worlds offered entry points to concrete issues of

- identifying our case in the context of a background or problem in our field;
- formulating research questions that are revisable; and
- designing a study—loosely, but not too loosely—in terms of particular times, spaces, and participants.

Those issues were embedded in and illustrated by our own studies of young children in pre-kindergarten, kindergarten, and primary grade settings. In addition, we addressed less concrete issues of researchers' roles and identities and how these influence the lenses we look through as we continue on the case.

Note

1. We thank Dr. Valerie Bang-Jensen, Saint Michaels College, Burlington, Vermont, for introducing us to this book and the parallel between Baylor and Parnall's story and the processes of qualitative research.

CHAPTER 4

Gathering Particulars: Data Collection

SITE AND PARTICIPANTS:

The site is one square block in a large city in the Northeast in a neighborhood known for its multicultural population and thriving small businesses.

Participants that have been identified thus far are a 5-year-old girl named Madlenka, her mother, her father, and her brother; these four are the key informants or participants. Others are residents of the block, named Mr. Ciao, Cleopatra, Mr. Eduardo, Mr. Gaston, Ms. Grimm, Ms. Kham, and Mr. Singh. All these participants have given the researcher permission to use their actual names. Additional participants will be identified when official data collection begins.

DATA SOURCES:

The primary sources of data for this study of intergenerational learning are observational field notes, audiotapes, and interviews.

Field notes. The researcher will observe Madlenka's block at different times of the day, writing in a two-column notebook, with a description of what is observed on one side and observer comments on the other.

Audiotapes. During her observations the researcher will audiotape conversations with participants, including

Madlenka and residents of the block who are acquainted with her. Equipment will consist of a digital audio recorder, with built-in microphone.

Interviews. Interviews will be recorded in two ways: informally during observations and formally once preliminary observations are completed and a range of participants are identified.

The above fictitious section on data collection is a much abbreviated facsimile of what researchers may write either as they plan their study or after they have completed it and are reporting their findings. The straightforward quality of the prose belies the complex decision making—and the degree of focus and time taken—that preceded the time of knowing whom and what to study. In this chapter we provide basic details about some common "hows" that enable us systematically to "get to know one thing as well as you can," in the old man's words (Baylor & Parnall, 1978, n. p.) .

GAINING ACCESS: PERSONAL AND INSTITUTIONAL STEPS

In the course of casing the joint and then moving on to create a design for a study, researchers hope that participants at the selected site grant permission to do the study. When the site is relatively autonomous, say, a community center, home-based day care, small private school, or city block, favorable conversations with administrators, residents, parents, or teachers may lead to permission to do the study (for a detailed and thoughtful description of this process in an early childhood setting, see Corsaro, 1981). This permission-granting is a critical first step and bodes well for the kinds of trusting relationships that underlie case studies that engage and inform both participants and researchers.

In some situations there are at least two additional steps to take before being officially on the case. First, in many school districts researchers may need to obtain the permission of a school or its district. School districts may have an office of research and their own procedures for submitting proposals for approval. Second, academic researchers need to obtain the permission of their college's or university's institutional review board (IRB), required by the U.S. government when research involves studying human subjects. Readers may be familiar with this process, which varies from institution to institution, and may encompass permission for studies ranging from term papers to doctoral-student and faculty-research projects. Whether these two kinds of approvals—from the research site and IRB—are requested in sequence or simultaneously also varies with the school district and academic institution. The process of obtaining the approvals may call for compulsively frequent communication with an advisor or administrative assistant.

When a review is required, hopeful researchers provide a description of the research purposes, procedures, and how their study will or will not change the routines at the prospective site. A challenge to researchers is describing these purposes and procedures in language that is clear to subjects or study participants. So while first-time researchers may be drawing on the academic discourse that their advisors expect, potential participants whose worlds are usually far from academe may find that discourse unclear and possibly alienating. Thus how we represent who we are in written form, particularly on the consent form that subjects/participants are asked to sign, has practical and theoretical implications. (For an example of how researchers proposing to study students of color in a public secondary school negotiated this dilemma as they worked within a multicultural feminist framework, see Knight, Bentley, Norton, & Dixon, 2004.)

Once the required permissions are in hand, researchers can turn to details of "official" data collection. By the way, a note to the anxious: The worries in the back of one's mind that participants will exercise their right, written into the consent form, to withdraw from the study if they wish are normal; but in the vast majority of studies that we have known about, the worries are needless.

FIELD NOTES: THE FOUNDATIONS OF THE CASE

No matter how much electronic technology we use to record what participants do in the spaces we choose to focus on, we still rely on field notes to construct a case. These notes are organic; they take on a life of their own and grow with the study over time. Ultimately they help to give an audience of readers a mostly verbal depiction of the site—an ethnographic sense of being in the world we call our case.

Ms. Yung's Room (Celia)

The first generation of notes (sometimes called "scratch notes" [Emerson, et al., 1995, p. 19]) might be extremely sketchy, especially if I want to observe more than I want to write while I'm in the classroom:

> Donna's room: 3/5/98—square room, lots of windows, light. Close quarters; rug area for circle, block area, housekeeping, library, computer, tables for art and math manipulatives (juice too)
> 8:50 Morning meeting—whole group.
> 9:15 Centers. Art: Ashley—2-fisted painter. Abstract painting red, dull green.

Sketchy though they are, the notes are *descriptive* and begin to capture a few essentials of a case study: time, space, participants, activity. Outside the classroom, these jottings could be combined with "headnotes" or memories to construct a more detailed account of particular events (Emerson, et al., 1995, p. 18).

Equally important as descriptive notes are those that go beyond what I observed. We have found categorizing different kinds of notes helpful in constructing descriptions and portraits of participants, contextualizing recorded talk, and planning next steps or mulling over what the data might be revealing. Bogdan and Biklen (2003, Chapter 4) suggest two categories, *descriptive*, which present as much detail as possible, and *reflective*, which might also be called observer comments. The content of reflective notes is virtually limitless but go beyond an objective description—based on our perceptions and observations of behavior—and relate to different aspects of the research process, such as ways of improving data collection or note-taking, analysis, or the dynamics of personal relationships at the research site.

In the study with Susan and Donna, I spent some time worrying about how best to audiotape children's talk. Thus the following would be a methodological note, written after a visit to the classroom:

> I'm worried about how we're going to get good-quality sound with all the usual background noise in a pre-k. Guess we'll have to try a few things, like a microaudiotape recorder. Where will we put it? Susan will have to hold it, and that would be tricky, since she'll be focusing on the children and writing, too.

In fact this idea was not a good one, as we never solved the problem of background noise and the frequent shifting of children from area to area during activity time, when opportunities for peer talk seemed greatest.

Moreover, my early vision of a study consisting of multiple case studies of *individual children* transformed into a case study of Ms. Yung's classroom, as readers already know. And ultimately our best record of what happened there was a set of videotapes that eliminated the need for detailed field notes at least regarding the focus of the video camera. Notes were still written about what we saw on videotape, as the tapes needed to be placed in a broader context and, later, within an interpretive context. With hindsight this was both a methodological and theoretical shift that required looking through a lens of a wider angle seeking out groups, not a lens that zoomed in on individual learners, or individual learners as foreground and their teacher, peers, or both as background. During data collection our case was composed more of a set of shifting, small social units than of the single larger unit of the classroom.

This shift from a metaphorical zoom to a wider angle lens was not fully captured in field notes, as it seemed to happen over time and with some diplomacy. That is, Susan may not have wanted to say directly at first that my idea about the audiotaping wasn't going to work. We had a number of conversations about the progress of the study, and I clearly remember listening to an audiotape of two children talking about a book. The audiotape was not clear at all, a discouraging fact. But the videotapes made of comparable contexts were clearer, even if they seemed less intimate in degree of detail about individual children. Here is a short excerpt from a transcript of peer book reading of *Hand, Hand, Fingers, Thumb* (1998), a book that Donna had read before to the class:

TIFFANY: (Ring those hands? Inaudible.)
JEFFREY: Dum, ditty, dum, ditty . . .
BOTH: Dum, ditty, dum, ditty, dum, dum, dum.
TIFFANY: There are friends, in the monkey's house(?)
(Susan's notes: Saying the words with a singsong voice the way Donna read the book to them, but the words are extremely hard to understand. They seem to be concentrating more on the way the words sound in rhythm, rather than what they actually are.)

My notes about this segment of the videotape follow:

It's hard to understand everything the kids are saying as they read in pairs with each other in this 9-minute segment. (A number of them are speaking to each other in Cantonese, which would be comprehensible to a Cantonese speaker.) Adam and Jacob are naming sea creatures in English and chatting too; Andy and Jenny, Sam and Tommy are animatedly speaking Cantonese much of the time. (This is the first time I've heard so much Cantonese from Tommy.) Except for Tommy's at one point spelling out T-R-U-C-K, the children are not reading in a conventional sense, but they are making meaning out of the printed texts while shifting their bodies, occasionally looking at the camera. (Peer reading looked very physical!) It's hard for me to focus on any pair of children because the camera is moving from pair to pair, sampling what each is doing. At 9:05 on the tape Tiffany and Jeffrey are playing with the sounds of the words "Dum dittie" and seem to be enjoying putting a lot of emphasis on "dum." At an earlier point on the tape Jeffrey said, "Give me a shake," to Tiffany and they vigorously shake hands. What's so striking about the whole segment is how playful all the children are and what a different view I get of them when they're talking to each other. I wonder whether I would have provided as broad and interesting a range of children's responses and behaviors as Susan did if I were videotaping.

Readers will see that in a collaborative study, field notes may contain descriptions, observer comments, and questions about the process of collecting data, provoked by a collaborator's particular focus or style. The short videotaped segment I described, in tandem with many other segments, could be interpreted as a demonstration of the social bases of early literacy. Thus it may illustrate how Susan's purpose for taping what she did merges with her theory about the importance of play and peers in spoken expression and early literacy.

Mrs. Kay's Room (Anne)

In my project in Mrs. Kay's room, these same kinds of notes appear. And I, too, construct field notes differently as my angle of vision changes. My formal field notes of whole-class lessons are transcriptlike, similar to those Celia constructed from classroom videotapes. Those of children playing are primarily descriptive narratives of what happened, supplemented with transcribed episodes to capture the content and interactional dynamics of the play.

Field notes of children composing are constructed through different kinds of data and take a unique shape. During the composing of one product, young children may be orchestrating different symbolic tools (talk, writing, drawing) and carrying on different conversations. The process is not only multilayered but also very quick and very "tiny," so to speak. That is, much interpretive sense can rest on whether a child made a particular comment before or after writing a certain word—it is the difference, say, between planning and evaluating. Similarly, the difference between "playing around during writing" and "playing through writing" rests on how exactly children's oral conversations relate to their written words.

To capture these fine-grained details, I use three different kinds of information as I construct field notes: (a) copies of children's products, (b) scratch notes, and (c) audiotapes. As we have already discussed, audiotaping in classrooms is challenging. To negotiate at least some of those challenges, I rely on how I position myself and my microphone. I sit behind and to the side of the focal child, so that I can see the child's mouth (which makes it easier to follow the talk) and the child's product. I use a detached, unidirectional mic, which gives me more flexibility than a built-in one. Although the children know I am taping (so that I can "remember" what they say, as I tell them), I keep the tape recorder itself in a tote bag and usually clip the mic to its handle. I can then slip the handle of the bag over a child's chair or on my own strategically placed shoulder or arm or even lay the bag on my knees.

I use the tape recorder to pick up the focal child's talk and any talk directed to that child, which will rise above the din quite naturally. Yet I cannot always determine from a tape to whom the child is talking, especially since young children talk aloud to themselves while composing; nor can I coordinate the talk with the writing. To provide these sorts of information, I depend on specially constructed scratch notes.

Extending an observational tool I appropriated originally from Graves (1973), I take scratch notes in three columns. In the first, I write words vertically as the child writes them; in the second, I use a code to indicate the nature (and direction) of the child's speech, composing action, or both; and, in the third, I write notes on nonverbal behavior and, also, the first few words the child speaks. If the child is drawing, rather than writing, I draw as the child draws, number the order in which objects are made, and circle numbers if there is accompanying talk. Following are sample field notes constructed from audiotape, scratch notes, and child products (a coding key is included at the end of the sample).

The Children are completing a template that reads *A ___ is a house for a ___*. Tionna is sitting by Ezekial.

Child's Text	Speech/Writing Code	Comments
	IS-P (Ezekial)	*Tionna*: You know what I'm going to write? "The sky is for Jesus." *Ezekial*: No. You mean "heaven." *Tionna*: No, "sky." You don't say "heaven". . . .
	RR	"A"
ski	OV	"sky"
	RR	"is a house for"
	IS-P (Ezekial)	*Tionna*: If you want to do something else, all you have to do is cross it out.
	/ / /	(Tionna crosses out the *a* on the worksheet.)
	RR	"A sky is a house for"
god	OV	"God"
	IU-P (Ezekial)	*Ezekial*: . . . You have to put a capital *G* for *God*. Because, look. It's a little tricky. You have to put a capital *GO* for *God*.
		Tionna: I know I do.

Key

Dialogue—IS-P: interaction solicited [by child author] from peer; IS-T: interaction solicited from teacher; IU-P: interaction unsolicited [by child author] from a peer; IU-T: interaction unsolicited from teacher or other adult.

Monologue—OV: overt language to self; RR: read or reread text; PR proofread (make a change in text);

Other—S: silence; P: pause; DR: drawing; / / /: erasing or crossing out.

As in Celia's project, my own theory about the importance of the intersection between child culture and symbolic tools draws my attention to certain aspects of the goings-on. My focus in this project is on children's appropriation and use of the traditional "basics" (including sensitivity to "grammar," clearly on display in the above notes). But, as the observations accumulate, I find myself drawn to the children's enacted friendships and their playful, sometimes reflective, ways with words (also on display). I pull child friendships and play out of the classroom din and lay them out against the quieter landscape of the page.

DOCUMENTING THE CASE ELECTRONICALLY

We sandwich this section on valuable equipment that some researchers use as aids in the collection and analysis of data between our discussion of field notes, based on observations, and a section on transcribing. The study of language and literacy has been transformed since the days of the durable and weighty reel-to-reel audiotape recorder. Now seen only in out-of-the-way closets or possibly in a 1950s television episode involving famed evidence-seeking lawyer Perry Mason, this artifact has been replaced by an array of audio and video equipment that enables instant and extensive documentation. Indeed, at times we feel that the process of moving data from one electronic site to another is enabled by a magician.

Accomplishing something that seems less magical to us, some researchers rely on electronic aids to record early jottings or in-depth field notes. Talking their notes into an audiotape or digital recorder or writing them on a handheld computer (personal digital assistant, or PDA) is an alternative to fast handwriting. Site residents might think that talking into a tape recorder is odd, though with the proliferation of cellular phones perhaps they wouldn't. Depending on the style of the recording device, researchers can save time because the written notes or digitally recorded sound can later be transferred/uploaded to a desktop or laptop computer. (Later in the data collection process, some researchers use digital video recorders.) Most case study researchers use an audiotape recorder so that they can revisit what was said at the research site. This seems indispensable in a classroom where one wants to "stop the relentless pace of the school day and think about what has happened and what has been said, again" (Ballenger, 1999, p. 84). Also indispensable is establishing a routine—nudged by stick-on notes or a watch alarm—of checking whether batteries are live and the recorder is working. Finally, regardless of methods of recording and storing data, make back-up copies of everything!

TRANSCRIBING IN TIME

Once begun, audio- or videotaping leads to at least two housekeeping challenges: systematic storage and timely transcription. Labeling tapes with the date of recording and an identifying number is a basic task that makes systematic storage possible. And solving the storage issue, given a safe container, shelf, or cabinet, is less daunting than keeping up with transcription. Ideally, transcription happens very soon after the tape is made, along with typing up field notes that provide the context for the contents of the tape. Because many researchers have day jobs and feel both fatigue and uncommon satisfaction after a successful data collection visit, they find timely transcription to be only slightly more probable than winning the lottery.

Still, the rewards for transcribing as data are collected are huge, and there are a number of ways to accomplish this. The first decision to make is about *how much* to transcribe. Some researchers think that complete transcription of all tapes is necessary, so they may cleverly force themselves to transcribe on a nearly daily basis. As she recorded Wally's and others' stories, for example, Paley (1981, pp. 218–219) owned only one audiotape, and so transcribed it faithfully each night after collecting data in her own kindergarten classroom.

Other researchers may make decisions at the research site to document and record only certain kinds of activities or interactions, depending on their research questions. In these cases everything that is recorded might be transcribed. If research questions are not so focused at the beginning of data collection, we might decide later in the process to transcribe selectively. So, for example, in a study of "the language of transitions," a researcher, to document the big picture, might audio- or videotape many segments of talk that are not obviously related to the phenomenon of making a transition from one activity to another. After careful listening, she may later choose to transcribe segments that seem related to transitions. Similarly, researchers collecting interview data may choose to transcribe segments of the interviews that are relevant to the questions shaping the case. (See Merriam, 2001, pp. 87–93, for a way of keeping track of key segments in an "interview log.") When deciding to transcribe only parts of a tape, we are aware that by saving time we may be overlooking data that deepen analysis later in the analytic process. Thus this decision to be selective is a trade-off that we would make reluctantly and pragmatically.

In addition to decisions about transcription, researchers have an increasing number of decisions to make about electronic tools that make transcription less time-consuming. A "low-tech" transcribing machine allows the researcher to manipulate tapes by operating a foot pedal to advance, reverse, or slow down an audiotape. Listening to the same piece of tape again and again when one's hands are free to type is not magical, but still saves on time and wear and tear on fingers.

Another potential time saver is voice-recognition software. This requires the researcher to "train" the software to recognize the recorded voice, whose speech is then transcribed by the software. This innovation is a particular boon for those who find typing difficult for any reason. If, however, a tape contains multiple overlapping voices, this technique will not work. In the end, completing transcriptions is a significant part of preparing and organizing data for analysis at the same time that it overlaps with the analytic process, detailed in Chapter 5. As we listen to or watch a tape for purposes of transcription, we inevitably begin to mull over the meanings of what we hear and type. That is, we begin to analyze our data.

Our analytic work is concretely reflected not only in what we choose to transcribe, but also in how we choose to represent our data on the printed page. Is the recorded conversation typed with one speaker placed after another, with turns of talk lined up flush with the left margin? Or is children's talk in a column of its own on the left side of the page, whereas adults' talk is in a column in the middle? Is there a third column on the right for researchers' commentary, or is the commentary inserted in parentheses in the columns of transcribed talk? Decisions about the look of the page are separable from neither our methods nor our underlying theories.

As Ochs (1979) explains, a transcript is an illustration of researchers' theories. That is, the conventional sequencing of one turn of talk following another from the top of the page to the bottom suggests a sequential theory of conversation: One turn is logically connected to the previous one, an assumption that most adults would make, especially if there is little written explanation of nonverbal behaviors or surrounding contexts. As one interested in children's language acquisition, however, Ochs (1979) points out that a very young child who is learning language will not necessarily say much and may not make responses that are relevant, at least from the adult's perspective. So a transcript that places the child's behaviors and contributions in a separate column on the left side of the page (the first side that is read by readers of English) could reflect a theory of child communication that is not entirely dependent on adult conversational rules. The child's contribution on the left shows the child as initiator, and thorough descriptions of her nonverbal behavior incorporate modes of expression that are not verbal. Such a view of transcript construction that blurs boundaries between organization/method and theory has implications for studying classroom talk, transcripts of which often aim to capture the vagaries of "learning" and acquisition of knowledge.

In an instance of English-language learning/teaching, for example, Ms. Yung could be seen as the source of knowledge in the following transcript:

During snacktime, Tiffany requests paper and at first Donna directs her to the writing center, but then realizes that this isn't what Tiffany means:

DONNA: You want a paper, Tiffany?

TIFFANY: Yeah. I wipe my hand!

DONNA: You want paper to wipe your hands? What do you need?

TIFFANY: Tissue.

DONNA: Okay . . . There are tissues behind you. Or do you mean a napkin?

TIFFANY: Napkin!

SUSAN: It's made of paper, though, isn't it, Tiffany?

DONNA: Yes, it is. A different kind of paper.

TIFFANY: (Holding up her napkin) Tissue.

DONNA: The tissue's right behind you . . .

TIFFANY: That is, um, nose. This napkin is wipe hands and that is for bathroom wash hands. (Points to the roll of paper towels in the corner)

DONNA: Paper towels! All different types of paper, right?

TIFFANY: Yup. (Genishi, et al., 2000, p. 72)

But if the transcript consisted of three columns (see Figure 4.1), readers might put Tiffany in the initiating role and Donna in an important, but not dominant, role.

The second transcript might reflect a theory that shows communication in Donna's room to be dependent on children's curiosity, agency, and abilities, which incorporate an English-language learner's nonverbal and verbal rules of communication. This is a less hierarchical, linear, and word-reliant theory than the one reflected in the first format. Both formats, however, illustrate how seemingly mechanical decisions are driven by researchers' theories and analyses.

In a related way, the three-column field notes of Tionna's composing reflect the theoretical assumptions that talk plays multiple roles in young children's composing and that oral and written language are dynamically interwoven in their efforts. For example, the coding of talk as self-directed overt

Figure 4.1. Tiffany Comes First: "Lesson" on Paper Rearranged

Tiffany	Ms. Yung	Contextual Comments
Yeah, I wipe my hand!	You want a paper, Tiffany?	During snacktime, Tiffany requests a paper and at first Donna directs her to the writing center, but then realizes that isn't what Tiffany means.
Tissue.	You want paper to wipe your hands? What do you need? Okay. . . . There are tissues behind you. Or do you mean a napkin?	
Napkin!	Susan: It's made of paper, though, isn't it, Tiffany? Yes, it is. A different kind of paper.	Susan inserts a clarifying question that repeats the "conversational theme."
Tissue.	The tissue's right behind you . . .	Tiffany points to the roll of paper towels in the corner and sums up the "lesson," using English forms that she knows.
That is, um, nose. This napkin is wipe hands and that is for bathroom wash hands.	Paper towels! All different types of paper, right?	

speech or socially interactive is part and parcel of the notes themselves. To conserve space in articles, Anne tends to present such data in a more conventional transcript style, reducing the composing actions to summary comments, as in the following:

> The children are completing a worksheet template that reads *A ___ is a house for a ___*. Tionna is sitting by Ezekial. She turns to him and asks,

> TIONNA: You know what I'm gonna write? "The sky is for Jesus."
> EZEKIAL: No, you mean *heaven*.
> TIONNA: No, *sky*. You don't say *heaven*. . . .

Tionna starts to fill in the template. She reads *A* and writes *ski*. She reads *is a house for* but does not read the next word [*a*], commenting to Ezekial,

TIONNA: If you want to do something else, all you have to do is cross it out. (She crosses out *a* and writes *god*.)
EZEKIAL: . . . It's a little tricky. You have to put a capital *GO* for *God*.
TIONNA: I know. . . .

The above format does indeed save space, but it also makes much less visible the self-monitoring and the complex orchestrating of symbolic tools and social communication writing involves. Moreover, it transforms a dynamic relationship between a child composer's own evolving text and her evolving interaction with a peer into a more subdued one, in which the writing is couched within the talk. But it would be just as accurate to suggest that the talk was couched within the writing, since it was Tionna and Ezekial's shared interest in a religious text that supported their interest in each other's efforts. Thus, the complex field notes support analytic work that may become invisible in eventual write-ups because of the exigencies of publication itself, including space. (We will return to write-up in our final chapter).

INTERVIEWS: THROUGH THE LENS OF PARTICIPANTS

The qualitative interview is a construction site of knowledge. An interview is literally an *inter view*, an inter change of views between two persons conversing about a theme of mutual interest. (Kvale, 1996, p. 2)

Much of what we want to know about language and literacy is embedded in observable everyday activities and transcribed conversations in the classroom or elsewhere. But since case study researchers seek multiple views on the world they are exploring, they also include data from interviews, on a continuum from formal to informal. At the formal end are interviews with questions established in advance, and at the informal end are interviews that resemble quick conversations. These might be queries about a just-audiotaped event in which a detail or an overall purpose was unclear to the researcher or a follow-up to something observed the day or week before. Thus researchers seek both to fill in gaps in their data and to hear about what is happening in participants' own words.

Because there are many books (e.g., Gubrium & Holstein, 2002; Kvale, 1996; Mishler, 1986; Seidman, 1991) and chapters (e.g., Bogdan & Biklen, 2003, pp. 94–104; Fontana & Frey, 2000) devoted to varied methods of interviewing, we include here a few illustrative examples of interviews that are linked to the sites and people we have been describing. Even the most formal interviews—scheduled in advance and with some guiding questions—are conversational and narrative in style. As supplementary data, they deepen an understanding of what we observe in the classroom and sometimes help to interpret observed activities from participants' perspectives. For example, in a formal and conversational interview with Celia and Susan about early literacy and assessment, Donna elaborates on the importance of blocks for young children, materials that she noticed were missing in many pre-kindergarten classrooms she was checking out for her 4-year-old son to attend:

> So you say, oh, we write a B. It's a line and a curve and a curve again. But if they [young children] don't know those words, like *half circle* or *curve*, not having the experiences from blocks, how would they see . . . [the letter shape]? . . . In the early years they need to be able to touch and explore, like the blocks and in the sand table. (Interview, November, 1999)

In her classroom, made up primarily of English-language learners (ELLs), she is always conscious of helping children to "know those words" that adults take for granted as they describe a letter's shapes and lines. Her comments about blocks reveal an underlying theory about how children learn, an instructional practice of teaching shape names in the context of hands-on activities, and a belief about how experiences that may seem disconnected from letters of the week undergird a budding knowledge of print.

Interviews with young children can also deepen understandings. Quick, informal conversations, right after a child finishes an activity or in an interactional lull, can be effective because researcher and child share a common reference point. Anne tends not to intervene this way, but does so when she is confused by a child's actions. In the following field notes, she reports beginning such an informal conversation:

> Tionna is bent over her drawing, talking to herself and drawing a traffic scene. She is coloring traffic lights red or green (and breaking the classroom rule about not coloring in the journals). Mrs. Kay says that children should start writing if they haven't yet, but Tionna keeps drawing and talking, describing vehicles, lights, and locations (e.g., "And here's the truck that hit us"). I do not know if this is a real or imagined scene:
>
> Ms. Dyson: Is that a true story or a pretend one?
> Tionna: A true. That's why I wasn't here yesterday. Was you here yesterday?
> Ms. Dyson: [I shake my head. "No."]
> Tionna: Me neither!
> Ms. Dyson: Because you were in an accident!?
> Tionna: I had to go to the hospital.
> Ms. Dyson: You had to go to the hospital!?
>
> Tionna returns to drawing, but Jon (a peer) has been listening. He asks, and gets answers to, a long series of questions, among them: "What happened?" "Were you hurt?" "What did your car look like?"

In its conversational style, the preceding interaction is typical of informal classroom interviews. That style reflects Anne's own position in the classroom, which was not one in which she pulled children off for special tasks nor, more generally, gave directions. Clearly Tionna, the "interviewee," felt comfortable asking a question herself, and Jon did not hesitate to interject his own questions. Nonetheless, Anne learned what she wanted to learn. The intense involvement in drawing (an intensity that Tionna, by this point in the year, displayed primarily during writing) seemed driven by a powerful personal experience and that experience seemed to lend itself more easily to visual than to verbal media. For some composing jobs, the "basics" of written language work against effective communication (i.e., linear displays are not good for conveying spatial positioning). In fact, it is just such an insight—that linear displays can work against analytic clarity—that has informed some of our own grappling with data collection and recording.

SUMMARY

In this chapter we have focused on some nitty-gritty "hows" of gathering particulars in the world that makes up our case. We addressed the following procedures and issues:

- Gaining access to the world we have chosen and obtaining the needed permissions.
- Collecting field notes as the foundation of our data.
- Recording language—spoken and gestural—as the core of interaction, using audio- or videotapes.
- Transcribing what is said, keeping in mind that part of this process is deciding how much to transcribe and what the format of the transcript means practically and theoretically.
- Interviewing as a supplement to field notes and transcriptions that captures the participants' views in their own words.

Our examples from the worlds of Ms. Yung's and Mrs. Kay's classrooms illustrated that gathering data is a process that overlaps with data analysis. Decisions about both intricate processes are inseparable from our theories about elements of the case.

CHAPTER 5

Constructing Assertions: Data Analysis

E thnographer Margery Wolf (1992, p. 129) writes, "Experience is messy." By the time that we as researchers are ready to focus on data analysis, messy human experience has become notebooks (and disk files) of typed field notes, bulging folders of artifacts of one kind or another, piles of (hopefully mostly transcribed) audiotapes, and other evidence showing that we have been there and done that work of gathering data. Our carefully bound case study—our effort to examine some phenomenon in some holistic social unit—has somehow lost its coherence. "Our job" now, as Wolf (1992) explains, is to search for "some coherency"; we are "not simply to pass on the disorderly complexity of culture, but also to try to hypothesize about apparent consistencies, to lay out our best guesses, without hiding the contradictions and the instability.

How in heaven's name do we do that?" (p. 129).

Indeed.

In this chapter, we will discuss data analysis, the process by which one transforms data (field notes, interviews, artifacts) into findings (assertions about a studied phenomenon that answer posed questions). In the sections ahead, we begin by highlighting key qualities of data analysis—its inductive and reflexive character. We then provide an overview of its typical procedures and common analytic tools, once again calling on Madlenka and her friends to help us explain their nature. Then we offer extended examples of data analysis, and to do so, we return to the classrooms of Mrs. Kay and Ms. Yung.

Searching for Coherency:
The Inductive and Reflexive Nature of Analysis

Imagine Liz, a young woman consumed by books—or, to put the matter differently, consuming many books (all for her research project on intergenerational and cross-cultural learning). Her piles of books are a constant source of bewilderment to her roommate, Megan, a fellow graduate student. One day, an unsuspecting visitor steps into their small apartment and immediately trips over and knocks down a precariously constructed pile of books, one of many stacks found throughout the abode. That visitor, Evan, a friend of Liz's, wants to create some logical order—some coherence—for these books by sorting them out (and maybe buying some bookshelves). He anticipates sorting them out by author, title, and subject, perhaps interrelating those three sorting (or coding) schemes in some way, and then rearranging the books in order to make some sense of the seemingly disorganized mess of books. When Liz goes out to find some take-out for lunch, Evan decides to surprise her by organizing the books in one corner of her living room.

Sitting in a corner of that apartment is the quiet, unassuming Megan. Acting against type, when the visitor starts to pick up his first book, she yells out, "Drop the book, Bub! You're messing up my project!"

Megan wants to create some coherence out of Liz's books too, but not by getting them off the floor—that is, not by pulling them out of their contexts. A budding qualitative researcher, Megan, like the visitor, might consider "a book" to be one kind of unit, one kind of piece of data, to be studied. And she also might want to know how that "unit of analysis" varies, including how each book might vary in author, title, and subject. But for now, driven by her case study of a graduate student's use of books (relative to other information sources), she wants to know how Liz herself has distributed the books throughout their apartment. As researcher, Megan is going to relate her analysis of the way books occupy the apartment's space with her analysis of the nature of the books themselves, along with other kinds of analytic work (e.g., studying book-using events in field notes and examining themes in interview transcripts, such as "access to information sources," "social networks," and "course work"). Megan is driven by larger assertions she is tentatively constructing about the importance of the physicality of books relative to other information media.

In this invented study, as in all qualitative case studies, the researcher's purpose is not merely to organize data but to try to identify and gain analytic insight into the dimensions and dynamics of the phenomenon being studied. That is, the end goal is to understand how the phenomenon matters from the perspectives of participants in the "case" (not, say, to the Dewey decimal system or any other kind of imposed category system). The process is inductive, grounded in the collected data—the artifacts (e.g., the books), the field notes on people's actions in particular contexts, and the interview transcripts of people's reflective talk. As pieces of data are organized and compared, as their variable natures are identified and named (or coded), as their interrelationships are examined, the researcher uncovers new spaces—new holes—in the developing portrait of the case, which need to be at least tentatively filled in; thus, new questions may take shape. Throughout this process, the researcher is driven by curiosity about the phenomenon—the researcher is on the case.

At the same time, though, the researcher's efforts are not simply "grounded" in the data (Glaser & Strauss, 1967). As the preceding chapters have illustrated, researchers have theoretical commitments (etic frameworks, as discussed in Chapter 2) and personal and professional experiences that inform all aspects of the project (Strauss & Corbin, 1990).

In other words, interpretive research is reflexive: Researchers' data gathering, analysis, and indeed, eventual write-up of others' experiences are mediated by their own lives. This reflexivity is, in fact, deliberately incorporated into the reflective memos that accompany field notes (see Chapter 3). And it is a part of the more intensive analytic work discussed in this chapter as well. To quote Dey (cited in Strauss & Corbin,

1990, p. 47), "[T]here is a difference between an open mind and an empty head." Researchers are sensitized to potential meanings of what is happening in some situation by knowledge of the literature and accumulated experience, both personal and collective (i.e., grounded in such societal forces as race, social class, and gender [Delgado Bernal, 1998, p. 563]).

In sum, the analysis of qualitative data is inductive, grounded in particular pieces of data that are sorted and interrelated in order to understand the dimensions and dynamics of some phenomenon as it is enacted by intentional social actors in some time and place. But the effort to understand others' understandings is mediated by the researcher's own professional, personal, and collective knowledge and experiences. These may become sources of hunches that can be systematically examined through the intricate detective work of analysis. It is through that analytic work that the inner workings of the case are constructed. In the following section, we provide an overview of the analytic procedures typically involved in analysis. In so doing, we will turn to the researcher now knee-deep in data gathered on Madlenka's block.

"HOW IN HEAVEN'S NAME . . . ?"
ANALYTIC PROCEDURES

It was exhilarating, if exhausting, to follow Madlenka around the block. It was even fun, if time-consuming, to transcribe the audiotapes of Madlenka's encounters with Mr. Gaston, Mr. Singh, and Mrs. Grimm. Now, though, Liz, the tired researcher, has an apartment full of tape cartridges; notebooks of field notes and interview transcripts; photographs of neighborhood shops and of much discussed objects (like Mr. Gaston's Eiffel Tower Cake); and, finally, piles and piles of books about socialization, immigration, play, and other topics that might inform her work. (Indeed, her apartment is such a jungle of books that it has inspired her roommate Megan's own research project.) Liz's job now is to systematically study her data in order to provide an analytic portrait of intergenerational and cross-cultural learning in Madlenka's neighborhood, an urban one containing a commercial zone populated by many immigrant businesses. Before beginning her work, Liz sketches out a rough outline of the analytic work to be done, as she currently envisions it. She needs to schedule time, first, to read through her data in chronological order. She anticipates later reorganizing the data so that it is separated by adult key participants (i.e., all the data gathered at Mr. Gaston's, at Mr. Singh's, and at Mrs. Grimm's); this reorganizing should further a comparison of the nature of adult-child interaction across sites.

After reading through her data, Liz plans next to begin the complex coding process. Through this process, Liz anticipates that her piles of data (if not her books) will be organized according to categories of cross-generational and cross-cultural learning as experienced by Madlenka and the adults. She also plans to do sociolinguistic analyses of "intergenerational events," so she can look closely at how Madlenka's relationships with her adult "friends" are negotiated through interaction. She will pay particular attention to any recurring ways of labeling, representing, or otherwise enacting the differences between the worlds of Madlenka and the immigrant adults. That is, she will pay attention to any discourse of difference—to ways of defining and enacting societal categories like age, culture, gender, and ethnicity (Foucault, 1978; Hall, 1997).

This analytic work should help Liz reduce her data set, since data will be transformed into examples of kinds of events or illustrations of important patterns or themes. Most important, as categories take shape, as Liz interrelates them within their contexts of occurrence and studies their relationship to thematic threads, she will develop a nuanced understanding of the nature and conditions of cross-generational and cross-cultural learning in this neighborhood of small shops and apartment buildings. Below, we elaborate on the key analytic work of coding and sociolinguistic analysis.

The Internal Dynamics of a Singular Case: Coding

Through analytic coding, researchers aim to figure out the conceptual importance of the human actions and reactions that have been inscribed in the data set. Discrete bits of data about individuals, behaviors, and contexts will become the discursive substance of analytic narratives about a studied phenomenon. In a sense, a researcher is developing the vocabulary needed to tell the story (or multiple stories) of what was happening in the case.

To illustrate the necessity of this analytic vocabulary, we borrow Erickson's (1986, p. 150) retelling of a familiar tale— sans the needed terminology:

> A young man walked along a country road and met an older man. They quarreled and the young man killed the other. The young man went on to a city, where he met an older woman and married her. Then the young man put his eyes out and left the city.

Following is Erickson's commentary, with some interjected remarks of our own:

> This version does not tell us about [or, in other words, does not use an analytic vocabulary that reveals] roles, statuses, and the appropriateness of actions, given those roles and statuses. The older man was not just any older man, but was Oedipus's father and king of the city. The woman was queen of the city and Oedipus's mother. Thus, actions that generally would be described as killing and marrying entailed patricide and incest.

Erickson directs readers' attention to the potential *social*, not psychological, meaning of what was happening. The findings of a case study in the interpretive tradition would not be a complex psychological portrait of a confused man but a complex social analysis of human choices and social actions, given particular cultural meanings and contextual contingencies.

A basic kind of work used to develop such a vocabulary involves inductive analysis of data. In this work, the basic unit of analysis is a piece of data (e.g., a section of field notes) that is meaningful or sensible on its own and that also contains a kind (or category) of information relevant to the study. In the initial open coding, researchers are, in a sense, brainstorming possible kinds of relevant information. They read through the data line by line, noting any words, phrases, or patterns of behavior that seem relevant. The goal here is to begin to probe beyond the behavioral descriptions, considering the social meaning or importance of what's happening. As Emerson and colleagues (1995, p. 146) suggest, researchers might ask of their data: What are people trying to do and through what means or strategies? How do people characterize others or their own situation? What sorts of assumptions about, for example, student-teacher relationships, institutional expectations, normal childhoods, or good families undergird their actions?

In open coding, researchers may mark significant passages in the field notebook and then write in the margins a word or phrase to describe the bracketed information. At the same time, they may keep a running list of all descriptors (and pages where they were recorded). Those terms can be reorganized—collapsed, eliminated, related hierarchically, or further differentiated—to develop a more focused category system for coding.

To illustrate, in a study of children's use of media stories in school composing and related dramatic play, I (Anne) marked all sections of field notes in which children explicitly referred to gender. In more focused coding, I compared these gender-related incidents, developing subcategories that identified certain characteristics or properties of the children's gender references and how those properties could vary. For example, the children's gender references had varying representational content (one subcategory). Within this subcategory, I listed and defined the varied human qualities that the children could explicitly refer to as gendered (e.g., physical appearance, emotional makeup, kinds of powers). Another subcategory involved the *functions* that reference to gender seemed to serve (e.g., to insult, to affiliate, to exclude).

I then used the analytic codes thus developed to study how children's representations and functional use of gender related to their decision making about composing and dramatizing stories. In this way I developed and studied the evidence for the assertion that the boys—the main superhero authors—tended to describe male superheroes in terms of physical powers and to describe female characters in terms of physical appearance. Further, boys only allowed girls who were similar to female media characters in physical appearance (including race) to assume certain roles; however, they did not restrict the male superhero roles to boys of similar appearance. Following is an excerpt from the project report:

> There was, of course, only one plum female role [in the *Teenage Mutant Ninja Turtle* stories]. Moreover, the physical qualities required by that role—slender, well-dressed, and white—seemed fixed. Thus, a girl like Tamara, a blue-eyed blonde whose poverty was as marked by her grooming as was [her peer] Seth's privilege, could never be an April and, initially, neither could a girl of color. Indeed, during composing time one day, Lawrence, who was biracial, commented to his peers that April *had* to be white. . . . At the very moment that he stated this rule, Lawrence was drawing Professor X—the bald, white leader of the X-Men superheroes—as a Black man with a flat top. (Dyson, 1997, p. 55)

I could have, but did not, frame the entire study as investigating the interrelated discourses of gender; race; and, less extensively, social class. Rather, I framed it as an ethnographic case study of primary grade children's use of superheroes (and other popular audiovisual material) in their play and literacy lives. Still, insights from the literature on discourse were part of the etic tools I brought to this inductive work (e.g., Foucault, 1978, 1981).

Language Events and Cultural Practices as Analytic Tools

In language and literacy studies, a fundamental concept is that teaching and learning, like other basic cultural processes, happen through socially organized interaction (Cazden, 2001; Mehan, 1982). And as we have stressed throughout this book, sociolinguists and ethnographers of communication have provided researchers with fundamental analytic tools for studying language interaction data. Classic studies in language and literacy education have used "speech" or "literacy events," "participation structures," topically related "episodes," "speaking turns," "communicative acts," and "functions" as units of analysis. These units are hierarchically related; for example, communicative acts, like question asking, take place within someone's speaking turn, which itself may be a part of a conversation (a kind of speech event).

In her groundbreaking study, Heath (1983) conducted case studies of three distinct cultural communities in one geographical area: a White working-class community, an African American working-class community, and a middle-class community, represented by the African American and White teachers in her college classes. By analyzing the kinds of speaking and literacy events constituting the language life in each community, she aimed to gain insight into the differential school achievement of the communities' children. Like many scholars of the time, she was interested in "mismatch" theories that emphasize the nature of discontinuities between language use at home and at school (Cazden, et al., 1972).

As part of her study, Heath (1982) paid attention to the *communicative act of questioning* as engaged in by parents and teachers; she focused on parent-child interaction in the teachers' homes and in those of the working-class African American children. Among the questions that undergird Heath's (1982) report are these: What is the nature of adult questions to children in the homes of children from these two different communities? What functions do these questions serve? What is the nature and function of teachers' questions to children in area schools?

Heath's teachers, who were students in her classes, helped her analyze data from their own homes. To clarify the analytic process explained in this chapter, we abandon all due humility and position ourselves in Heath's imagined work area, surrounded by her data. We have already read through "our" data. Indeed, we have identified what seem to us theoretically rich events or episodes, in which differences in the uses of questions seem strikingly evident. But we do not have a language for talking about these differences—indeed, we have not even systematically examined our data to see if our "sense" of informants' "sense" is sensible, so to speak.

So, to begin our analytic work, we organize the field notes, which contain transcribed audiotaped interactions, by site (i.e., those collected in the home and in school) and by cultural community. We read through the data, identifying all "question-asking" episodes. We do not simply pull out the questions, because without the contextual information provided by the episode, we would not be able to determine the questions' functions nor how the children responded to them.

In our analysis, the communicative act of questioning is one kind of unit of analysis; we compare each contextualized instance of questioning, inductively developing a taxonomy of kinds of questions, distinguished by the kind of response they were to elicit and, for each question category, the functions it might serve. By considering our data through the lens of these taxonomies, we generate assertions about differences in questioning between the studied cases. For example, in the homes of the teachers, parents asked children many questions that could be called "known-answer questions," precisely the kind that dominated in school; these questions seemed to socialize children to be experts on the names and attributes of people and things surrounding them, including those introduced through books. In the African American children's homes, in contrast, adults tended not to ask such questions but, rather, to ask for analogies (i.e., "What's that like?") or to invite stories.

In her discussion of her assertions about differences in question asking, Heath considered evidence from both her sociolinguistic analysis and her thematic study of her field notes, particularly those sections in which parents and teachers commented on their own or "others'" use of questions. For example,

> [a] grandmother playing with her grandson age 2;4 asked him as he fingered crayons in a box: "Whatcha gonna do with those, huh? Ain't dat [color] like your pants?" She then volunteered to me: "We don't talk to our chil'un like you folks do; we don't ask 'em 'bout colors, names, 'n things." (1982, p. 117)

Thus, Heath interpreted her data by relating variation in language use across settings, supporting her assertions about differences in question-asking practices with related information from the perspective of varied project participants. Her interpretation was reflexive, mediated by the theoretical inclinations she brought to her work and her personal experiences as a local educator. She thought in terms of the social, cultural, and linguistic space that separates children's homes and schools and aimed to contribute to bridge-building.

A decade later, new notions of language and culture were gaining ground in educational case studies. The influence of "practice theories" helped transform "culture" from a set of beliefs and values to a social dynamic organized within and by interconnected practices. These practices are resources that individuals draw on, produce, and, potentially, transform as they respond to structural conditions (e.g., of race, class, gender) and local contingencies of everyday life (Bakhtin, 1981; Hanks, 1996; Ortner, 1996). Moreover, in these newer conceptions, culture is "put in motion," as Rosaldo (1989) discusses, and so are individuals. Thus, children in complex urban environments are not necessarily only participants in singular cultural communities. Children's oral and written language may reflect this diversity, as they appropriate interactional resources from diverse cultural sites (Dyson, 1993, 2003; Vasquez, Pease-Alvarez,

& Shannon, 1994; Zentella, 1997). (Of course, even within any one community, age, gender, class, and ethnicity may all matter in how one participates in cultural practices.)

Culture in motion, individuals participating in transcultural events, resources accumulated in lives that cross borders without even packing a suitcase or booking a flight—these ideas are circulating in our invented researcher's head, too, as she contemplates the data collected on Madlenka's block. Indeed, reading about these concepts informed her own decision to focus on "intergenerational and cross-cultural events." And so, pencil in hand, legal pad poised (like us, she can be quite retro in her technological tools), she pushes aside a few library books and makes space on her desk for her field notebook and gets to work.

We have been working too. Our offices, like that of Madlenka's researcher Liz, are filled with what might seem "ragtag collection[s] of facts and fantasies" (Wolf, 1992, p. 129)—field notes, interview transcripts, children's products, and curricular documents—all of which need to be woven together to construct "the case." That is, like other case study researchers, we are "maker[s] of quilts," aiming to assemble images that probe the nature of our respective phenomenon (Denzin & Lincoln, 2000, p. 4).

Our studies are ongoing—we are still adding to the "collection," so to speak; and our cases are complex, with multiple narrative and analytic threads. Below, we each pull on one strand of those threads. These are elements of our respective cases—two "cultures in motion," filled with socially organized interactions quite different from those on Madlenka's block. In our studies, children and adults step into the social and cultural units called Ms. Yung's and Mrs. Kay's classrooms and in so doing cross generational, cultural, and educational boundaries that often go unanalyzed. Readers will notice that the analytic strands we ask them to follow are woven in different ways, as we illustrate contrasting and complementary styles of analysis and presentation. So now, without further ado, we invite you to step first into Ms. Yung's room.

Ms. Yung's Curriculum (Celia)

Stepping into Ms. Yung's classroom is typically an action accompanied by sound, namely, the sounds of children talking, sometimes loudly, and of adults doing the same. At every moment we are aware of the challenge of documenting "messy human experience," to use Anne's phrase, especially when threads between the official and unofficial curriculum are purposely entangled. As presented elsewhere (Genishi, et al., 2001; Genishi, et al., 2000), Ms. Yung's pre-k curriculum is an integrated one in which spoken and written language are continually interwoven; and definitions of reading and writing include emergent and child-constructed understandings and behaviors. Thus language arts basics in this pre-k room are not often discrete and lesson-based. Instead, the omnipresent basic of spoken language gives shape and form to a fluid curriculum.

Recall from earlier chapters that we three collaborators had an underlying concern with the extent to which pre-k curricula were under pressure to become academic or focused on basics. That concern was a tacit backdrop as we zeroed in on how Ms. Yung and her children enacted a broadly integrated curriculum—the abstract phenomenon that is enacted in our case. More specifically, we began with a look at how her children's vocabulary developed. After 4 months of the school year had passed, though, Ms. Yung observed that vocabulary and spoken language didn't seem to be a driving curricular focus. She noted a greater focus on social goals, so that classroom talk was as much about how to behave in groups as it was about the ELLs' English vocabulary. Despite this observation, a chronological look at stacks of transcripts, field notes, and conversations with Ms. Yung revealed vocabulary learning/teaching events that appeared in varied and numerous contexts. Guided by our research questions, we culled these events from the sometimes tangled threads of classroom life; and because Ms. Yung most often participated in them, they had the look and feel of official pieces of the pre-k curriculum.

In the following sections I focus on a single conversational event to illustrate some ways of analyzing that highlight both pedagogical and sociolinguistic aspects of what is said. Although the overall goal of our analyses is to construct holistic case studies, an interest in vocabulary learning and teaching can lead to analyses that take on a linear and decontextualized look. Readers shouldn't fret—the coding process, through which we reduce the data set, will still retain threads to a developing narrative, elaborated upon later in Chapter 6.

The prelude to an extended conversation between Ms. Yung and pre-kindergartner Tommy is a short chat between him and Susan. They talk about Tommy's drawing, which he has made after looking at *Goodnight, Moon* (Brown, 1976). Ms. Yung then takes a seat at the art table across from Tommy. The two learn about where the other lives, and along the way Ms. Yung offers a conversational mini-lesson on English vocabulary. She also later learns what Tommy knows about some sounds and their corresponding letters—the alphabetic principle demonstrated. In Figure 5.1 the conversation appears on the right, and coding indicators and notes appear on the left. Numbering in the transcript is arbitrary; it enables me to refer to a specific line that may or may not be a "linguistic unit."

During this conference Ms. Yung sustains both the conversation and what she later called her assessment of Tommy's knowledge of sounds. I present this 9-minute interaction, much longer than most interactions between Ms. Yung and a child, in order to illustrate ways of segmenting and analyzing that vary depending on the theoretical frame or research question we are foregrounding. And like any transcript, this one changed a bit as I watched the videotape and then listened one more time to the audiotape. So much is said, sometimes simultaneously, that an additional hearing often leads to adding or deleting a word or clarifying the order in which something was said.

The additional hearing also leads to insights about ways to code this stretch of talk. As we said earlier, the initial open coding is a kind of global brainstorming. How can we describe what we think is going on here? For starters, we are coming

Figure 5.1. Tommy and Ms. Yung's Conference

Coding Ideas	Transcript	
Whole	Ms. Yung:	1. Whose house is this? What a nice
conversation		2. house!
1–171	Tommy:	3. Somebody's.
• child originated	Ms. Yung:	4. It's somebody's house? Is it Tommy's
• curric. assess.		5. house?
	Tommy:	6. It's not mine. My house is bigger!
1–29	Ms. Yung:	7. Your house is bigger?
• vocab. lesson/	Tommy:	8. Yeah. This is my house here. (He
contrasts		9. draws an apartment building.)
• teachable m.	Ms. Yung:	10. Oh—your house is in a building.
		11. So where do you live? Which floor
		12. do you live? Right there? Is
		13. that the window?
	Tommy:	14. Yeah, that's mine. This here.
	Ms. Yung:	15. That's yours there?
	Tommy:	16. Yeah—1, 2, 3, 4, 5,
		17. 6, 7, 8, and 9. Whoa—
		18. 9!
19–29	Ms. Yung:	19. That's a big building!
• child direction		20. Yeah, that is a big house, building.
		21. You live in an apartment, right?
	Tommy:	22. Nope.
	Ms. Yung:	23. That's called an apartment. When
		24. you live in a building like that,
		25. it's called an apartment.
	Tommy:	26. No, I live that way (thinking D.
		27. pointed in the wrong direction
		28. toward his apartment, he points
		29. in the opposite direction).
	Ms. Yung:	30. Oh, sorry, that way. So
		31. in an apartment. Who lives in the
		32. apartment with you, Tommy?
	Tommy:	33. My mom.
	Ms. Yung:	34. Your mom, and who else?
vern.	Tommy:	35. My grandma, but she go away.
	Ms. Yung:	36. Your grandma . . .
vern.	Tommy:	37. She go away.
	Ms. Yung:	38. Your grandma went away? Your
		39. grandma went to China, right?
		40. How about Grandpa?

Figure 5.1. (cont'd)

vern.	Tommy:	41. He's go away too.
	Ms. Yung:	42. So it's just Mommy and Tommy right
		43. now?
	Tommy:	44. Yeah, just me. It goes this way
		45. (said while drawing windows
		46. on his building).
47–94	Ms. Yung:	47. I like your building. Do you
• letters-sounds		48. know your address?
• teachable m.	Tommy:	49. I know.
	Ms. Yung:	50. You know? What is your address?
	Tommy:	51. 9-D!
	Ms. Yung:	52. 9-D? You live in apartment 9-D?
		53. Can you write 9-D on your
		54. drawing somewhere, so we
		55. know that is your apartment?
	Tommy:	56. I think I'm going to draw this.
		57. D-d-d.
	Ms. Yung:	58. Nine D. Do you know how to write D?
	Tommy:	59. I know.
	Ms. Yung:	60. Do you know the address? What's
		61. outside? The outside number. That's
		62. inside. What's outside? What's the
		63. name of the street when you walk down
		64. the street? What street you live on?
		65. What street is it: Catherine Street,
		66. Henry Street, Madison Street?
	Tommy:	67. Madison Street.
	Ms. Yung:	68. Madison Street? You know how to
		69. write Madison? (Tommy nods "no.")
		70. OK, I am going to say the word
		71. Madison—muh.
	Tommy:	72. M!
	Ms. Yung:	73. Mmaaaaa—
	Tommy:	74. Mmaaaaa—R!
	Ms. Yung:	75. Duh duh—maduh—
	Tommy:	76. D!!
	Ms. Yung:	77. OK, sonson—suh
	Tommy:	78. Son—S.
	Ms. Yung:	79. Maadisonnnn. Nuh.
		80. (Tommy has written *M-R-D-S* on the
		81. right side of the paper,
		82. vertically, starting with *M*
		83. on the bottom and ending with *S* on
		84. the top.)

Figure 5.1. (cont'd)

Ms. Yung:	85.	Look. I see the street. *Madison*.
	86.	Very good. What number? Is there
	87.	a number outside?
Tommy:	88.	Inside.
Ms. Yung:	89.	Is it 44, 40, 46 Madison?
Tommy:	90.	I don't know.
Ms. Yung:	91.	You don't know? You go
	92.	home—you take a look today,
	93.	OK? There's a number—on the
	94.	building outside.
Tommy:	95.	There's a sign right here.
	96.	I'm going to make a sign.
Ms. Yung:	97.	You're going to make a sign? OK.
Tommy:	98.	The sign is—a 100.
Ms. Yung:	99.	One hundred? That's the sign?
Tommy:	100.	Ten!
Ms. Yung:	101.	Ten? What sign's that for?
Tommy:	102.	The sign for go fast.
Ms. Yung:	103.	Go fast? Oh, only go 10 miles per
	104.	hour. Only 10 miles.
	105.	You know what, Tommy? I live
	106.	in this kind of house (points
	107.	to houselike structure in
	108.	his painting). Not a big building
	109.	like that. A small house,
	110.	like that. That's my kind
	111.	of house. That how my house
	112.	look like. And you know
	113.	what's my address?
Tommy:	114.	I don't know.
Ms. Yung:	115.	I show you what my address
	116.	look like. Can I write right here?
	117.	Or on a different piece of paper?
Tommy:	118.	Write 'nother paper.
Ms. Yung:	119.	OK, I'll write on another paper.
Tommy:	120.	You can write backwards (flips over
	121.	his sheet of paper).
Ms. Yung:	122.	I can write backwards? OK, I'll write
	123.	my address (writes her address
	124.	on the back of his paper).
	125.	The number of my house is 12.
	126.	Can you read this word?
Tommy:	127.	I don't know.
Ms. Yung:	128.	12 Bantel Road, that's my address.

116–124
• child direction

Figure 5.1. (cont'd)

	129. And yours is Madison, 9-D.
Tommy:	130. 9-D Madison, 9-D.
Ms. Yung:	131. Yup. Very good. And go 10 miles.
Tommy:	132. New York, New York.
Ms. Yung:	133. New York, New York. Write that?
Tommy:	134. Yeah, two New Yorks.
Ms. Yung:	135. Two New Yorks? OK, you want to
	136. write New York, New York
	137. then. Where? Where you
	138. going to write it?
Tommy:	139. Right here.
Ms. Yung:	140. Right there? You want to write over
	141. here? (pointing to a different spot)
	142. Give you more space?
Tommy:	143. But my house is here (points
	144. to right side of paper).

145–161
• *letters-sounds*
• *teachable m.*

Ms. Yung:	145. OK, your house is here. Let's
	146. make more space. OK, go ahead.
	147. New York. Nnnnew, Nyuuuuu.
Tommy:	148. Nnnnnnew—nuh—N! (writing in
	149. the middle of the paper,
	150. not along the bottom where
	151. Donna had earlier pointed)
Ms. Yung:	152. OK! Ewuuuuuuuu.
Tommy:	153. U!
Ms. Yung:	154. OK.
Tommy:	155. Yuhyuhuh—
Ms. Yung:	156. Yyyyuhuhuh—
Tommy:	157. I don't know. E!
Ms. Yung:	158. OK, New Yoooork. Kuh.
Tommy:	159. R!
Ms. Yung:	160. R? New York. Kuhkuhkuh.
Tommy:	161. Yeah, OK, New York.
Ms. Yung:	162. New York, I can see it. Madison
	163. Street, Madison 9-D, New York,
	164. New York. You read it to me.
	165. Where's Madison—
Tommy:	166. Madison—
Ms. Yung:	167. Where's Madison?
Tommy:	168. —street, 9D, New York.
Ms. Yung:	169. Wow! This is a beautiful writing.
	170. Can I hang it up?
Tommy:	171. OK . . . .

in on the middle of something. Recall that Tommy has drawn a picture, and he and Susan have chatted about it briefly. Ms. Yung then enters the scene and starts what she calls a conference with him. So we could begin with a preliminary code or category (hand-written on my own coding sheet) for the whole conversational event: it is a "child-originated" piece of the curriculum, which would not have evolved without Tommy's interest in *Goodnight, Moon* and his related drawing.

From Tommy's perspective (actually, mine as a researcher, since I didn't consult with Tommy on my analysis), this conference is an opportunity for extended attention from Ms. Yung. For the most part, he seems eager to cooperate, to answer her questions and show whatever he knows about print. He also has candid responses to some of his teacher's questions; for example, when she asks if she can write on his paper, he at first says no and then changes his mind (lines 116 through 124). And he reads her actions, inferring at line 26 that she is indicating the location of his apartment building, and corrects her by pointing in the opposite direction. Thus we can bracket lines 19 through 29 and infer that Tommy took Ms. Yung at her word: When asked, he can make the choices he wants, and it is also all right to correct her if she is wrong. The focused code or subcategory for both those segments might be "child direction." In addition to the "basic" of talk, then, children's choices, for example, to draw a picture during activity time, are central to the structure of this pre-k curriculum. In the following sections we see how through talk Ms. Yung builds on Tommy's choices and introduces other basics of vocabulary and early literacy.

Finding Pedagogical Units

Although Tommy's choices anchor this whole conversation/conference, Ms. Yung's abilities to build curriculum are notably woven throughout. In this sense, the conversation could be an example of the teacher's curriculum building, interwoven with informal assessment. Thus, I might add to the coding column "curric-assess" as a second open code or category for the whole interaction.

Within the conversation, many other analytic possibilities are shaped largely by our collaborative research questions and partly by the hierarchical nature of language. Our driving questions have to do with what is learned and how Ms. Yung is teaching, though each of us might define learning and teaching in slightly different ways. Thus a logical next step in coding might be to ask, Are there specific "language lessons" that Ms. Yung and Tommy accomplish here? And are they embedded in shorter conversational units within the identified longer unit? One shorter unit is the initial conversation about the differences between the words *house, building,* and *apartment.* So I might focus on lines 1 through 29, putting a bracket around them, to the left of the previous bracket, perhaps writing "vocab lesson" or "vocab contrasts"—a subcategory—close to the new bracket.

Further, because Ms. Yung has talked with Susan and me earlier about the importance of "teachable moments," I might code the same section (lines 1–29) twice, adding "teachable m" to the margin. Next, I might ask where other teachable moments begin and end, as I focus on how Ms. Yung structures what we could term her pedagogical or instructional work. For example, between lines 47 and 94 there is an extended embedded unit that we could title "Do you know your address?" Ms. Yung is shaping another teachable moment—a piece of the curriculum—while she confers with or informally assesses a particular child. She confirms that Tommy already knows letter names and in this situation can match some of them to sounds, depending on their location in a word. (A similar moment occurs between lines 145 and 161.) However, he does not demonstrate knowledge of the convention of writing in English from left to right, horizontally across the page. Still, Tommy demonstrates a unique interest in and knowledge of print, relative to his classmates. *High/Scope* (Hohmann, Banet, & Weikart, 1979), the published curriculum for pre-k that Ms. Yung adapts according to the school's policy, is not prescriptive in terms of what she should do next; thus what unfolds between Ms. Yung and Tommy in a conversation about his drawing is woven into her individualized pedagogical goals.

Finding Embedded Sociolinguistic Units

This lengthy example illustrates one way in which the basic of talk unfolds in Ms. Yung's room, offering rich and numerous analytic possibilities. Within its layered discourse are multiple teachable moments; there may also be embedded units of social or sociolinguistic work. For example, if we are interested in the *communicative act of questioning*, as Heath (1983) was in her study, we could revisit the pieces of talk around questions and do more focused coding. In a third analytic round starting at the vocabulary lesson/teachable moment between lines 1 and 29, I might use a fresh photocopy of the transcript to avoid confusion and indicate questions with arrows in the coding column. (Readers can imagine the arrows and mentally insert possible codes.) Ms. Yung initiates the conversation about Tommy's drawing with a question, to which she probably does not know the answer. She already knows, though, that like most of his peers Tommy lives not in a house, but in a large apartment building near the school. What, then, is Ms. Yung communicating through her acts of questioning? Up to line 21 when Ms. Yung asks her 10th question, "You live in an apartment, right?" her questions seem to "show interest" and "sustain talk," providing opportunities for Tommy to describe his drawing. At line 23, Ms. Yung converses in a way that is familiar to teachers who are doing the kind of pedagogical work that offers information—about the word *apartment*—and also leads to the following bracketed unit that we earlier called "Do you know your address?" Thus an analysis focused on what Ms. Yung communicates through her many questions becomes quickly interwoven with her pedagogical and social goals; a sociolinguistic analysis that focuses on communicative acts and how they function is not separable here from acts of teaching.

Looking less at function and more at form, we can identify utterances (as in line 50) as questions because of intonational or grammatical features." You know?" has a rising intonation at the end, as do most questions in English. And in "What is your address?" the use of a *wh-* or question word followed by an inversion of the subject (*address)* and verb (*is*) signals a question.

Attention to these features constitutes *linguistic* analyses or analyses of *questions as questions.* They may also connect to potential research questions that are related more to participants' language than to Ms. Yung's language arts program. For example, we might ask what Tommy, an ELL, has already learned about the syntax of English. In line 35 he says, "My grandma, but she go away," not the conventional/standard syntax of English speakers. Similarly, in line 41 he says, "He's go away too." These utterances could be analyzed from a prescriptive point of view (that is, measuring them according to standard adult usage); or they might be placed within a sociolinguistic frame in which we acknowledge vernacular differences in the English of bilingual Cantonese-English speakers. (I've written "vern" in the coding column to indicate some of Tommy's different uses.) Any analysis of his vernacular forms is complicated by his youthfulness and his status as an ELL. His "errors" might be those of most 5-year-old children learning English. They might be developmental and drop out of his repertoire over time; or they might reflect features of Cantonese (in which tense is not marked with specific inflections or endings, as it is in English or in Romance languages). A researcher interested in young children's acquisition of verb forms might meticulously document changes in Tommy's syntax, as well as that of other ELLs in Ms. Yung's room. However, in the broad universe of possible research questions, collaborative analyses with Ms. Yung and Susan consistently turned toward the pedagogical.

An Analytic Quilt: Are There Patterns Developing?

It's clear by now that researchers' questions shape the analytic process, at the same time that the data themselves suggest ways of analyzing. In the conversation between Ms. Yung and Tommy, I suggested a number of ways of segmenting and coding their talk. And readers recognize that there are multiple other threads they might have followed had they been given the data. They might also differ with me about exactly where embedded units begin and end. Threads begin to come together when *many* examples like the one above are analyzed and common threads are found; that is, some of the categories and subcategories identified above will frequently recur. As important, contrasting threads are studied that incorporate aspects of a less official curriculum and push on the boundaries of the developing case. So as I proceed, I would take care to analyze contrasting examples of interaction, perhaps illustrating Tommy's talk with children. For example, he demonstrated his fluency in Cantonese when speaking with friends who shared his home language. More to the point, since I asserted that Tommy was unusual, I would look to other children's actions and talk to illustrate how much the children varied in their language-learning styles and rates. The analyzed examples should illustrate that by the end of the school year, many children were becoming comfortable with English, while a small number of children were just beginning to speak it. Also, as a group they showed a general interest in print, as when Ms. Yung read to them, but individually most children did not focus on specifics, like letters of the alphabet.

Further, the children in Ms. Yung's room varied as persons negotiating a complex social space, for many their first space shared with a peer group. Tommy, for example, may have shown an unusual interest in print, but he also displayed unusual exuberance. Thus his family was more concerned with his louder-than-average voice and greater-than-average talkativeness than with his growing knowledge of letters and sounds. Perhaps his family looked to Ms. Yung to provide social guidance before she got to academic goals. I would analyze, then, examples from children with differing social styles, those children whom Ms. Yung painstakingly drew out and encouraged to speak English or to engage with texts of different kinds. In other words, I would seek to represent the case fairly, presenting examples that confirmed and disconfirmed my preliminary analyses. The analytic quilt under construction should make evident details of Ms. Yung's curriculum that are meaningful to child and adult participants alike.

This search for multiple meanings raises more questions and leaves threads dangling. We make room for the expected, presumably incorporated in our research questions, and the un-expected, what we glean because we remain open to multiple interpretations of the events we've documented. So in response to the overall question about how an integrated curriculum is enacted in Ms. Yung's room, we might tentatively formulate this assertion, based on analyses of numerous teacher-child in-teractions: In Ms. Yung's room, children could originate activities that the teacher took up in *teachable moments*, blending un-official with official pedagogical goals. *Pedagogy* incorporated social as well as academic content.

In the following chapter, I come back to discuss how this assertion might relate to others and to Ms. Yung's beliefs—her ideology—as well as how the assertion might fit within the broader framework of early childhood curricula and school-ing. For now, though, Anne is motioning for you to come into her office. (Watch your step.)

Piece Work "in" Mrs. Kay's Class (Anne)

I am no longer literally in Mrs. Kay's class, but for all practical purposes I have not left. I still hear the voices of Mrs. Kay, Ms. Hache, and the children, not only when I re-play my audiotapes, but also when I read through my field notes or study a child's product and a scene replays itself in my mind. My "presence" in Mrs. Kay's room, though, does not feel the way it did during data collection. I am not fo-cused on gathering information to stretch or deepen my par-ticipation in and observation of my case. Rather, I am hon-ing in now on my data, organizing my gathered materials according to my ever more finely articulated (or so I hope) research questions.

In truth, though, the whole process feels much messier in the doing than any neatly printed prose could convey. The analysis is often channeled—or temporarily diverted—by late-night hunches. Those hunches are spurred by a response to long evenings of field-note reading, and they are followed by intense data searches, which end as the sun comes up. In other words, there are hunches; flashes of insight (or otherwise); and deliberate, systematic analysis.

In constructing my case of Mrs. Kay's room, I aim to understand how young schoolchildren—growing up amid cultural, linguistic, and semiotic diversity—are learning to write in a time of curricular standardization and concern for the so-called "basics." To this end, I have lately been concentrating on my field notes. I began with a general open-coding of my field notes, identifying recurrent themes in the data (e.g., gender, friendship, media references). Then, anxious to get to the supposed heart of the matter, I read to identify the "basics" themselves. I developed categories to name those basics, that is, those aspects of language and language use that received recurrent teacher attention (e.g., grammatical usage, capitalization conventions, and spacing). This, however, was hardly the heart of the matter. That is, this descriptive analysis of the teacher's focus was necessary but not sufficient for understanding how she and the children were perceiving writing instruction.

To probe more deeply into participants' frames of reference, I changed my own analytic focus. Rather than concentrating on a "basic" as a primary unit of analysis, I decided to step back a bit and use the emic notion of a "fix-it"; this was Mrs. Kay's term for a problem in a text that needed to be fixed. Grammatical usage, for example, then became a kind of fix-it, or "problem." I could thus ask, inside official classroom composing events: What kinds of fix-its did the teachers attend to and with what evaluative discourse (i.e., with what implicit or explicit ideological perspective on language)? In their official or unofficial composing times, what problems did the children attend to and with what evaluative discourse?

To answer these questions, I have begun identifying recurrent classroom composing practices, including teacher modeling of the writing process, children's "journal" composing, and editing conferences. In so doing, I am reducing all "official" teacher-led literacy events to varied types. Once the data are so organized, I can analyze them for their focus (i.e., what "basics" receive much attention) and the routine structures of

events, including any language routines and evaluative discourse (e.g., "How can we say that better?"). I also need to
organize the data by focal child, so that I can examine each
child's participation in official and unofficial events—and each
child's composing problems, the times when they decide an
already planned or written text needs some adjustment.

In doing this work, I can follow the threads of official fix-
its—like grammatical usage—through varied kinds of composing events, seeing how they fade in and out of attention
and even come into conflict. Already I am beginning to select
key events that, when transformed into narratives, are richly
entangled with the project's analytic threads and thereby bring
those threads together in dynamic ways.

With all this tangling and untangling of threads, the current text is in danger of becoming tied in knots. So I will call
on Tionna, her teachers, and her friends to help me demonstrate the complex process of analytically constructing a case
of teaching and learning the basics. I begin with two kinds of
data featuring Tionna: a journal entry (written in February)
and related field notes (which contain audiotape transcripts as
well). These data are intermeshed in order to construct one of a
series of linked key events—an editing event, a kind of official
composing practices:

The editing conference begins with Ms. Hache's request
that Tionna read the following text to her (see Figure 5.2 for
Tionna's original piece of writing):

> Lyron is the best boy in the
> class he is cute to me and Janette
> ~~we will both live with him~~
> when we grow up me and Janette
> like him he side [said] oh pless [please] he
> is very cute to me and Janette.

Although Ms. Hache will attend to all of Tionna's perceived errors, she zeroes in on that coordinated subject, "me
and Janette."

Figure 5.2. Tionna's "Lyron" Text

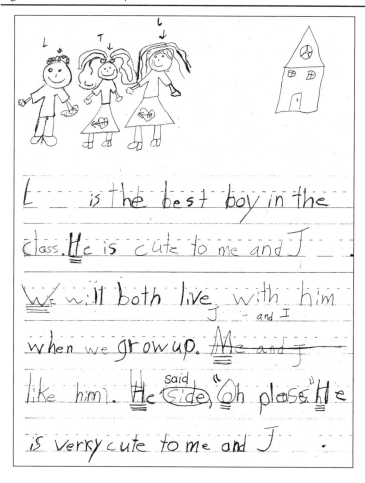

Ms. H.: How can we write "me and Janette" different?
(And when Tionna does not respond) We do it every
morning, sometimes [in a daily sentence correction
exercise]. "Janette and [pregnant pause]." What's another way to say "me"? (No response is forthcoming).
One letter.

Tionna: You? [u]

> Ms. H.: No. "Janette and . . ."
> Tionna: I.
> Ms. H.: So right up here write "Janette and I."

And Tionna does so.

When Tionna and Ms. H. are finished with their conference, Tionna's text reads as follows (changes are in bold):

> Lyron is the best boy in the
> class. **He is cute to me and Janette.**
> **We** will both live with him
> when we grow up. **Janette and I** [crossed out *"me and Janette"*]
> like him. **He said "Oh please."** **He**
> is **very** cute to me and Janette.

Grammatical usage is one subcategory of problems to be fixed. This thread is evident in teachers' actions and, moreover, in documents such as the official district curriculum, the proposed state benchmarks, and the standardized achievement test. On her own, though, Tionna rarely problematized grammatical usage, and she did not do so in composing the "Lyron" piece. However, she did focus on another problem, one identified by Lyron himself.

I did not hear this new problem as a "problem" when I was focused on the conventional basics. But once I stepped back and began to consider fix-its, I noticed this other subcategory of writing problems, quite different from "grammatical usage." I could "hear" it in the field notes I composed for Tionna's composing of the "Lyron" piece.

Tionna's journal event began with her drawing of herself and Lyron. When she was done, she said, "Now there's me and Lyron. I'll write about me and Lyron and all them next time." However, Lyron, sitting across from her, made it clear that *he* wanted "all them" in her story *this* time.

Lyron had confronted Tionna with a kind of fix-it, a writing problem centered on social relations. To understand the problem involving "all them," I needed to interrelate the fix-it thematic thread with those related to friendship and unofficial "gender play" (after Thorne, 1993). The field notes on these themes clearly document the long-standing but complex relationship between Tionna, Lyron, Janette, and Mandisa.

Indeed, these children had been showing up in one another's journals since the beginning of the year, as they were friends. In the winter months, though, when playing "girlfriends and boyfriends" was spreading throughout the unofficial world, the children at times redefined their relationship. This is exactly what had been going on the day that Tionna wrote her "Lyron" text. The play had begun before journal time, when Lyron and Tionna sat playing Legos together. Tionna had been building her home when Lyron implicated himself into her house!

> TIONNA: This is my small room 'cause I got parts to my
> house. Soon as you walk in there's a part right there—
> LYRON: My picture's on the wall, when you walk in.
> TIONNA: Yeah. This is *my* room, and this is my living room.
>   . . .
> LYRON: Where's *my* room?

The location of Lyron's room is settled and, then, Tionna explicitly states what has now been implied:

> TIONNA: I'm marrying Lyron. I *will* marry Lyron. I will
> *marry* you Lyron. I will. . . . Me and Janette will. Then
> you'll have two girlfriends. You know Janette likes
> you.

And Lyron agrees:

> LYRON: Both of you guys can marry me.

When the children return to their seats for journal time, Lyron again begins the play:

LYRON: (Turning to Tionna, who sits across from him) I know what you're gonna write about.
TIONNA: What?
LYRON: Me.

At this point, then, I return to Tionna's journal event. When framed in the light of unofficial relations and play practices, Tionna's problem becomes clear: She is leaving out her friends and, moreover, her companions in the gender play. As the event continues below, Tionna has included Janette in her drawing:

TIONNA: (Drawing) Now there's me and Lyron . . .
LYRON: And Janette.
TIONNA: Me and Lyron and Janette—nobody else.
LYRON: Mandisa! (i.e., "Don't forget about Mandisa," who sits at the other of the two classroom table clusters, unlike Tionna, Lyron, and Janette)
TIONNA: She'll be in there next time.

Tionna did not fix her drawing and writing to include Mandisa; her eventual written piece included Lyron, Janette, and herself—"nobody else." But near the end of the year, when I asked Tionna to reread this piece for me, she tripped up on Ms. Hache's editing for grammatical usage and seemed to recall having actually edited her text to include her good friend Mandisa.

TIONNA: (Reading) "Lyron is the best boy in the class. He is cute to me and Janette. We will both live with him when we grow up. Me, Janette, and I, and Janette—Me, Janette, and I" (pause).
Ms. DYSON: I think that's where [the teacher] was doing that editing.
TIONNA: (sigh) "We will both live with him Janette and I when we grow up. Me, Janette and I and Janette!" . . . Supposed to be Mandisa in there too. And I did—did

[inserted] like him. "He said, 'Oh please!' He is very cute to me and Janette." Where's Mandisa? I ain't put her name in there just once.

Ms. Dyson: . . . Why would Ms H. and Mrs. K. cross [those words] out?

Tionna: I don't know.

Any textual improprieties, much less social ramifications, of "me and Janette" (the grammatical fix-it) did not seem clear to Tionna, but leaving her good friend Mandisa out of the "like" play (the relational fix-it)—that was another matter.

At this point, then, I have taken primarily one analytic concept—the fix-it—and have begun to identify how it might vary (its subcategories), the situational (or event) circumstances in which particular fix-its become salient for some classroom participants, and key pieces in my analytic quilt that bring many kinds of threads together. Already I am formulating some rough assertions about the basics: The official world's fix-its were focused on traditional written language conventions and undergirded by a hierarchical notion of language—there are "better" ways of saying things. The children introduced the horizontal notions—in certain relational circumstances, there may be better choices of what to say and how to say it. Further, I am already thinking that, for grammatical usage conventions, a hierarchical view of language does not capture what Tionna and, indeed, most of Mrs. Kay's children would need to do to say things "correctly." If certain grammatical forms are not developmental errors (which "me and Janette" could be) but vernacular differences (which seems likely, given Tionna's use of African American Vernacular English), horizontal code-switching for relational purposes is what, in fact, Tionna would need to do to meet the school's requirements (Smitherman, 2000).

I can hear in the preceding paragraph how my interest in illustrating the piecework of data analysis is being overtaken by my desire to engage in the work itself. Celia and I both can get quite wrapped up in our data, and we both at times wonder: How do we know it's time to stop finding new questions and thus stop analyzing? When do we know we've pulled on enough threads—induced a sufficient number of categories, themes, statements, or pedagogical or other ideologies?

Recurrence or repetition is often an indicator, as is the sense that we have seen a particular theme or category many times in varying contexts or with different participants. And we know that constructing a case study from numerous, sometimes disparate, themes and ideas depends not only on messy coding processes that are exhaustive (and exhausting) but also on due dates or longed-for graduation dates. So although each of us would like to write "The End" in oversized letters as the final words of our study, we know that there are threads that could be pulled and pursued well beyond that place and time.

Still, we have not yet arrived at our "The End" points. So we are going to put this book aside for a while and spend some time hanging out in our respective bounded realities. Below, we take a proper leave by closing the chapter with a brief summary and a bit of advice.

Resisting Neat Narratives

In this chapter, we have illustrated the processes through which analytic order is constructed from the messiness of everyday experience. Among these processes are

- close reading of field notes and other gathered data;
- developing analytic codes to group pieces of data into categories of relevant information;
- using sociolinguistic concepts to analyze how teaching and learning are socially organized and enacted;
- noting recurrent terms, statements, and ways of talking that represent and construct societal differences; and
- interrelating analytic categories with situational circumstances and participant perspectives to develop assertions about "what's happening here" relative to the phenomenon of interest.

Through these processes, researchers weave together different pieces of data into a patterned quilt, an interpretive case study. The pieces themselves, now coded, are bits of participants' social actions; accounts of recurrent events; and explicit or implicit indices of historical, societal, and institutional contexts. Thus, there are characters, settings, plots, and grand themes, and, when they are woven together, there are narrative accounts of who did what, how, and in what circumstance.

Such narratives allow researchers to bring together many different analytic elements into a familiar, comfortable form. But that familiar coherence can also be a problem. There are often competing stories for the same happening, not because some are "the truth" and some are not, but because participants are differently positioned in relationship to teaching and learning; they have different agendas, different ideologies of what is right or appropriate for "school," for "children," and for language use itself. Moreover, people are seldom of one "mind," so to speak, nor of one "identity" (Gilroy, 1997; Hall, 1997). As contextual situations change, as the circulating discourses change, people change too, just as Tionna and Lyron transformed themselves from friends to each other's (nonexclusive) betrothed.

Through analysis we are not on the trail of singular truths, nor of overly neat stories. We are on the trail of thematic threads, meaningful events, and powerful factors that allow us entry into the multiple realities and dynamic processes that constitute the everyday drama of language use in educational sites. What's "basic," then, becomes a matter of perspective, of what's foundational from the point of view of the participants we study. It is, in fact, the competing stories, put into dynamic relation with one another, that allow insight into participants' resources and challenges and, moreover, into the transformative possibilities of social spaces for teaching and learning. In our final chapter, we consider the ways in which case studies themselves contribute to the educational community's efforts to transform classrooms and schools to better serve children and youth.

CHAPTER 6

Making a Case Matter:
On Generalization

Whenm Madlenka's parents ask her where she's been all day, she says, "Well . . . I went around the world. And I lost my tooth!" (Sis, 2000, n.p.). Is Madlenka overstating the case? Can she (over)generalize in this way? After all, researcher Liz has carefully documented that her primary participant has gone around exactly one city block. So however vivid Madlenka's intergenerational encounters with friends of diverse cultures have been, readers might argue that this small space cannot constitute "the world." And is our informant implying that the whole world is interested in her lost tooth?

Interpreted as a case (which it is not, of course), Madlenka's experiences can be made to speak to a diversity of issues, including one of the thorniest: generalization. We propose that her individual experiences—and the sense she makes of the world around her—are part of a constructed case of intergenerational learning that is at once particular and general. Our invented researcher Liz would weave the particulars of Madlenka's block and the people on it into the broad contexts that she has learned about through personal experiences, her files of data, and the stacks of books in her apartment. Thus the construction might foreground Madlenka's own perceptions and those of her friends, contextualized within recent immigration patterns in this neighborhood and others or within economic trends that enable intergenerational friendships between Madlenka and local merchants. Weaving together the contextual threads so that a quilt of persuasive images—a coherent narrative—emerges is the goal of case study researchers.

In this chapter we address the complexities of moving from particulars to the general, as Liz might have done. First, we consider basic notions of "generalization," as they figure into case study methodology. In so doing, we move from our consideration in Chapter 5 of assertions about the case (e.g., the intergenerational enactment of Madlenka's world) toward those that situate the case in broader professional conversations about the phenomenon itself (e.g., the nature of intergenerational learning). Second, we draw on varied studies to illustrate how case studies have both contributed to and complicated generalizations about language and literacy teaching and learning. Indeed, in more recent scholarship, the very notion of a neatly "bounded" social unit has been rendered problematic, with consequences for how researchers, like Liz, construct their case studies.

Finally, we step back from the "loose teeth" of our own studies and their categorized particulars of separate analytic threads and discuss how we aim to weave case study quilts that matter. Moving from analysis to interpretation soon entails the transition from painstakingly writing notes and analyses to writing a paper, article, or chapter. Because there is already much published about "writing it up" for different audiences (Bogdan & Biklen, 2003, Chapter 6; Clandinin & Connelly, 2000, Chapter 9; Erickson, 1986; Richardson, 1990), we do not offer details here on that process. Instead we focus on how we might write up the "discussion and conclusions" sections of our respective studies (i.e., how we might "wind it up"), as a way of thinking with readers about how particular case studies may assume broader professional relevance.

GENERALIZABILITY: ON MATTERS OF TRUST AND RELEVANCE

When Madlenka tells her parents she's been around the world, they surely consider the source and the context in deciding how to interpret her words. Matters of source and context—more particularly, matters of trust—are central to the concept of generalizability. At its core, this concept has to do with researchers' relationship to an eventual audience. How do researchers, so concerned with particular people in particular circumstances, construct case studies that have relevance beyond the case itself?

In Chapter 5, we considered how researchers analyze their data to formulate what we might deem, after Stake (1995), a kind of *propositional generalization*—assertions about how a studied phenomenon was enacted in a case. We imagine that among Liz's assertions was that Madlenka's relationship with each shopkeeper was based, at least in part, on her interest in appealing objects that caught her eye (and her nose, we must add)—among them, Mr. Gaston's baked goods, Mr. Singh's candy and colorful books, and Mr. Ciao's ice cream truck. In the "findings" section of her own paper, Liz grounded the assertion in detailed evidence, itself constructed from varied kinds of data.

For example, from her observations and interviews, Liz knew which shopkeepers Madlenka addressed by name (and vice versa); she knew something of the history of Madlenka's relationships with the shopkeepers through her interviews with them as well as with Madlenka's parents and Madlenka herself; from her audiotapes, she knew common topics of conversation between Madlenka and the merchants, particularly those focused on, or emanating from, Madlenka's interest in the shopkeepers' goods. Liz even had a marvelous drawing Madlenka made in which Paris's architectural wonders were parts of pastry items; the Eiffel Tower, for instance, was a cake decoration. This interrelated detail, based on varied categories of information (e.g., shops on the block visited and not visited, topics of conversation, representations of shopkeepers' countries of origin), helped Liz construct assertions with "interpretive validity," that is, assertions that seemed reasonable and trustworthy about the local meanings and social dynamics of Madlenka's intergenerational encounters on her block (Erickson, 1986, p. 150).

Those very details might be pivotal in allowing readers themselves to generalize to the world beyond Madlenka's block. This is, after all, what we human beings do: We respond to present circumstances, at least in part, by relying on the relevance of past experience. In this way, the world becomes a more orderly place, and we become more sensible in our actions, having, after all, the wisdom of experience. So if a study gives readers a sense of "being there," of having a vicarious experience in the studied site, then readers may generalize from that experience in private, personal ways, modifying, extending, or adding to their generalized understandings of how the world works. This might be referred to as *naturalistic generalization* (Stake, 1995).

However, our imagined researcher Liz, akin to our own researcher selves, also aimed to construct propositional assertions that situated her analytic work on Madlenka's block in larger professional discussions about intergenerational learning. In other words, she wanted to move from case-bound, past-tense assertions about what *happened* to present-tense assertions about what *happens*. To illustrate, our imagined researcher Liz wanted to move from an assertion like

> Madlenka's relationship with each shopkeeper was based, at least in part, on her interest in appealing objects.

to something like

> Informal, intergenerational relationships may originate when adults and young children meet through the local pleasures of childhood—for instance, sweet treats; bright, handheld objects; and magical stories.

Moving from a generalization about a case to an ahistorical assertion about a phenomenon itself—the dynamics of its process, influential factors in its enactment, and issues that may arise—requires intellectual space, so to speak (Becker, 1990). And this is because the findings of any qualitative case study are not replicable per se; they are a concrete instantiation of a theorized phenomenon. By understanding the particulars of its social enactment (e.g., the relationships entailed, the thematic content and interactional details of its unfolding, the specifics of time and place), the case can be compared to the particulars of other situations. In this way, "truths" or assumptions can be extended, modified, or complicated.

In our imagined case, Liz was generalizing about the process of intergenerational and cross-cultural relationships and learning, not about what children learn from immigrant shopkeepers. She would have been hard-pressed, in the latter instance, to analytically situate her research in the literature, since, of course, there would scarcely be literature. Moreover, she was generalizing about a dynamic process that undoubtedly would be realized differently in different circumstances, in different cases.

In the "discussion and conclusions" section of her paper, Liz concentrated on situating her study's findings in the literature; she used those books still scattered through her apartment to help her compare her case to related cases and to the literature more generally. In this way she could strengthen her findings about factors that shape intergenerational learning in dense, commercialized neighborhoods like Madlenka's. Moreover, she hoped that allowing insight into these factors, and the potential for young children and adults to enrich each others' lives, might be useful to educators, community workers, and neighborhood planners (for examples of such a discussion based on case studies of preschools, see Corsaro, 2003).

In a seminal publication that appeared more than 30 years ago, Hymes (1972c, pp. xviii, xiv) articulated how this sort of generalization process could be useful to, and contributed to by, practitioners themselves:

> The point here is that to stress the importance of the participants in a situation is a matter, not of courtesy or rhetoric, but of scientific principle. To understand language in its social context requires understanding the meanings that social contexts and uses

of language have for their participants . . . and [researchers] of language are to a large extent in the same boat as participants in classrooms in this matter. . . . [Research] papers may offer helpful perspectives and insights, but for them to be effective in a classroom, they must be articulated in terms of the features of that classroom and its community context. . . . These papers can suggest new things to notice, reflect upon, and do . . . [but] [i]n the last analysis, it is the understanding and insight of those in the concrete situation that will determine the outcome.

Since Hymes published his reflections, there have been many studies of very particular cases that have informed how we as educators and researchers pay attention to classroom situations. However, there have also been professional disagreements about individual studies and about the methodology itself.

On Collapsing Cases and Blurring Boundaries

Conflicts about case study research have allowed insight into how, and through what kinds of professional dialogue, case study research may contribute most powerfully to education. Generalizability has been central to these professional controversies.

Sometimes the controversies evolve because the conceptual distance between a phenomenon and a case—so basic to generalizability in qualitative case study research—seems to collapse. The detailed "case" (e.g., a studied teacher's pedagogy, a child's learning history) becomes the "phenomenon" (e.g., effective teaching, writing development). For example, a study of a young child's early literacy learning may conclude with a description of "stages" or set behaviors to be expected from other children, who may be learning in other social and cultural contexts and whose actions may be contingent on other material and human circumstances (Dyson, 1999). A study of the specific procedures of specific teachers in specific classroom settings may give rise to instructional scripts to be used by all "effective" teachers, no matter what their curricular possibilities (Reyes, 1992). It is as if a study of intergenerational learning on Madlenka's block led to the pedagogical implication that little children should traipse unaccompanied around the neighborhood informing others of significant events. The detailed work of case study research thus detracts from, rather than contributes to, the analytic, comparative construction of knowledge.

At other times, conflicts arise because the theoretical underpinnings of qualitative case studies are misunderstood or simply incompatible with policy goals. As noted in Chapter 1, such is the case currently, as the federal government aims to identify "scientifically proven" teaching methods. Since singular case studies do not aim to determine context-free associations between methodological input and achievement data, their contributions to teaching and learning can be dismissed (Jacob & White, 2002).

In the end, readers "make their own sense of [data] fragments even though the note-taking ethnographer created, selected, and arranged them in the text" (Emerson, et al., 1995, p. 209). Readers' "sense" is likely to be informed by the discourses—the systems of articulated social knowledge—through which they understand such social constructions as "culture," "school success," and "good parenting." A dramatic example is provided by the Heath (1982) project discussed earlier (see Chapter 5).

Heath situated her work in developmental sociolinguistics. Against that backdrop, she argued that her findings about the verbal strategies, including the questioning, in her comparative case studies of different cultural communities led to the broad assertion, the generalization, that ethnographic data on community language use was necessary in order to effectively teach children from outside the defined cultural mainstream. To develop this generalization, she used her data to problematize assumptions about "easy" (e.g., known answer) or "hard" (analogy) questions about school texts. Such determinations cannot be abstractly determined, she said, but depend on familiarity to the children. Like other language and literacy researchers working at the time (e.g., Au & Jordan, 1981; Moll & Diaz, 1987), she explicitly rejected the belief that teachers had to "enrich the background" of so-called nonmainstream children because their "differences" worked against school success (1982, p. 126).

Nonetheless, in a highly influential summary of reading research, Heath's work was used to support an assertion about "other" parents who fail to provide children with appropriate experience "playing school-like question and answer games" (Anderson, Hiebert, Scott, & Wilkinson, 1985, pp. 23–24). The niceties of sociocultural research—issues of patterns and demands of daily living, of differences in life rhythms and routines and resources—were apparently irrelevant, although clearly they are central to qualitative case studies. The familiar paradigm of evaluating children's home language practices in the light of schoollike ones prevailed.

The way in which case studies of "cultural differences" were recontextualized as explanations of school failure led to concerns that within case studies, minority communities in particular were being essentialized. That is, they were displayed as separate, parallel worlds, defined by characteristic behaviors, not as internally complex groups, situated within and as part of the larger society. From this critical view, "cultural differences" are produced as academic difficulties within schools, in part because of habitual, routinized (i.e., hegemonic) ways of organizing instruction and evaluating learning (Erickson, 1986; McDermott, 1987).

In current case study research, the boundaries around social groups are more often seen as constructed between groups, shaped by history, ideological clashes, and power struggles. In Ortner's (1999, p. 9) words, "The point is not that there is no longer anything we would call 'culture,'" but that interpretive analysis of social groups should be situated "within and, as it were, beneath larger analyses of social and political events and processes." This seems to us important for any qualitative study of a social unit. A case, be it a community, a classroom, or a program, is not a separate entity but a located one, existent in some particular geographic, political, and cultural space and time. Not only is this blurring of boundaries evident in studies of social groups, it is evident as well in the study of individuals. As Rosaldo (1989) explains:

> More often than we usually care to think, our everyday lives are crisscrossed by border zones, pockets, and eruptions of all kinds. Social borders become salient around such lines as sexual orientation, gender, class, race, ethnicity, nationality, age, politics, dress, food, or taste. Along with "our" supposedly transparent cultural selves, such borderlands should be regarded as . . . sites of creative cultural production. (p. 207–208)

Given the complexity of individuals' lives, Erickson (2002) proposes "the daily round" as a unit of analysis, in which researchers identify the varied interactional practices that constitute an individual's everyday life. Although they did not use the term "daily round," in *Pushing Boundaries*, Vasquez, Pease-Alvarez, and Shannon (1994) do use this notion in their case studies of children in a Mexican immigrant community in northern California. They were interested in how individual children's social networks involved their participation in many "intercultural transactions" or events (another kind of data piece or "unit of analysis"). Children drew on multiple sources of linguistic and cultural knowledge to participate in these events, be they conversations with people outside the Mexicano community or instances of cultural brokering, in which they translated for family members in varied institutional settings.

Through their case studies, the researchers aimed to problematize the tendency to view Mexican immigrant children's home lives as somehow oppositional to school and to support an assertion that immigrant children may develop flexible repertoires of linguistic resources as they negotiate their needs and desires in their daily rounds. They situated their findings within the literature on Mexican immigrant communities throughout the United States, which may afford children similar opportunities. A child's daily rounds was also at the heart of Liz's imagined study of intergenerational and cross-cultural learning. And Madlenka's block—like many sites in these times of mass media, transnational workers, and refugees—does not allow an easy linkage of place, culture, and identity (Gupta & Ferguson, 1997). Clearly, Madlenka's block cannot be understood apart from its place in larger structural and societal dynamics. Still, Madlenka *has* traveled around a very particular world, one seen from the confident perspective of a young child who seems urbane as well as urban. Our notions of bounded social units may need some updating, but, to repeat Geertz's apt words (1996, p. 262), "no one lives in the world in general."

In our final sections, we turn to our own particular case study worlds, the real ones we have entered in Ms. Yung's and Mrs. Kay's classrooms. We briefly discuss our efforts, planned and completed, to make those cases matter.

Ms. Yung's Curriculum: Moving from Assertions-in-the-Case Toward Generalization (Celia)

Being on the case in Ms. Yung's classroom meant putting analytic boundaries around her free-flowing integrated curriculum, a social unit full of child- and teacher-originated content. In our previous accounts of aspects of the curriculum (Genishi et al., 2000; Genishi et al., 2001), we presented numerous examples of children's and Ms. Yung's talk, although our purpose was not primarily to explore meanings of *integration*.

Like Madlenka's researcher Liz, I propose case-bound assertions about what happened in Ms. Yung's room, reviewing the assertion introduced in Chapter 5 and adding two more. All three are drawn from collaborative analyses of many examples of activity-based talk, usually between Ms. Yung and a child; interview data; and artifacts that illustrated how the phenomenon of an *integrated curriculum* was enacted in a very particular location:

- In Ms. Yung's room children could originate activities that the teacher took up in *teachable moments*, blending unofficial with official pedagogical goals. *Pedagogy* incorporated social as well as academic content.
- Child-originated activity incorporated children's choice of multiple language(s). Official pedagogical goals did not include, then, "speak English by the end of the year."
- Children took up "basic" pedagogical goals, such as demonstrating phonemic awareness in English, at different points in the year, with an unusual child like Tommy showing a high level and other children showing a moderate or not yet observable level of phonemic awareness.

A reader who has worked with young children may have private responses to these case-bound assertions, for example, articulation or modification of her or his own understandings, what Anne referred to earlier as *naturalistic generalization* (Stake, 1995). From our point of view, this is a much desired response, as we would want Ms. Yung's practices to speak directly to others.

Researchers, however, seek to move readers beyond the specifics of a single case, here Ms. Yung's curriculum, to assertions about the phenomenon itself. This abstract move could be illustrated with the following propositional assertion:

An *integrated curriculum* may be defined by a significant degree of child choice, including choice of language used in the classroom, and by teachers' corresponding flexibility in setting pedagogical goals.

This definition of *integration* is anchored in the specifics of a single case, so it points back toward the past-tense assertions about Ms. Yung's room. At the same time it points toward the present, toward contemporary issues in early language and literacy education.

Discussion and Conclusion

It is these issues that I would lead up to as I pull together the analytic strands in the "discussion and conclusions" of this case study. The beginning of this section might sound like this:

> I return to the long interaction between Ms. Yung and Tommy, pulling together several strands that illustrate what *integration* means in the world around these pre-kindergartners and their teacher. There is a quality of seamlessness to this conference that would have evolved very differently without Tommy's drawing, an outgrowth of his interest in the picture book *Goodnight, Moon* (Brown, 1976). The extended focus on Tommy's apartment building incorporates counting/math, whereas the later focus on letters and their sounds is clearly related to literacy learning. But the academic "inserts" are embedded in conversations that are integrative in a more social than pedagogical sense. Ms. Yung offers information about her own home and address, and, in response to her questions, Tommy tells her about his grandparents' absence at his apartment.

Next I would restate that Tommy was unusual, referring back to the many contrasting examples from other children's interactions with one another and Ms. Yung. As I noted earlier, many children were comfortable speaking English at the end of the school year, but a number were just beginning to speak it. As a group, they showed interest in print generally, though individually they did not focus on specifics, like letters and sounds.

I might later raise the question of what the range of child styles and behaviors suggests about Ms. Yung's ideology—her beliefs about teaching, learning, and how both influence children's lives in their community. So I might continue the discussion in this way:

> As for Ms. Yung's ideology, it too is integrated, in the sense that it consists of multiple approaches to teaching, not just one. Her beliefs about teaching and learning are traditional enough to allow her to impose teachable moments, which may or may not be taken up by the learner. Her own words reflect an eclecticism that combines pedagogical requirements, such as letters of the alphabet, and a firm belief in child-led exploration:
>
>> So you say, oh, we write a *B*. It's a line and a curve and a curve again. But if [young children] don't know those words, like *half circle* or *curve*, not having the experiences from blocks, how would they see . . . [the letter shape]? . . . In the early years they need to be able to touch and explore, like the blocks, and in the sand table. (Interview, 11/99)

In this collaborative study, the words of the pre-k teacher herself lead up to final points about current issues in early literacy education.

Ms. Yung's justification for an integrated curriculum matches well the overall ideology of many early childhood educators (see Bredekamp & Copple, 1997, for example). In the light of the educational present, however, some early childhood educators might judge Ms. Yung's ideology to be "traditional" or out of date because they accept the current shift toward teaching academic skills. Pre-kindergartners are increasingly pushed to spend more of their school lives learning the "basics" of letters and sounds (see Brenna, 2003, for a description of how an emphasis on literacy skills has changed the Head Start curriculum). Thus what Ms. Yung says about the importance of child exploration and the traditional staples of early childhood curriculum, like blocks and sand, talks back to a simplistic view of what is *traditional* or *basic.*

For instance, close looks at the basic of spoken language, illustrated by the many conversations we recorded in the study, push the boundaries of the curriculum beyond literacy, art, math, and other subject matter content. Casual questions about Tommy's grandparents reflect interest in the learner, but also serve to incorporate familial and cultural knowledge into the curriculum as it unfolds through talk. Because parents, grandparents, and other family members—along with the language that most of them speak—have been welcome in this social and educational space, Ms. Yung knows the local culture. She knows whether someone is taking a vacation in China or is responding to a family health emergency; she knows which parents work long hours in local businesses and which work at home. And she can imagine what impact the particulars of children's lives might have on the way the curriculum unfolds. Thus the boundaries of our case are not neatly contained within Ms. Yung's crowded room. Indeed the real-life quilt on display in Ms. Yung's school, with its weaving together of bold colors, patterns, pictures, and print, represents the spirit of Ms. Yung's curriculum and ideology more fully than a written summary of her "curriculum content."

Further, the messiness of boundaries in our case provides a striking contrast with reductionist views of the basics of literacy instruction, reflected in a long-running debate, sometimes called the "reading wars" (Allington, 2002; Garan, 2002). That debate has focused on the politics and practices of teaching reading in holistic versus discrete, phonics-based ways. At present, discrete approaches dominate in literacy and language education, as practices in Mrs. Kay's room illustrate. According to Ms. Yung, there was and is pressure in her school district to adopt these discrete, academic approaches, to focus specifically on letters and their sounds in English.

Thus the phenomenon that we have identified as Ms. Yung's integrated curriculum talks back to the redefinition of early literacy as narrowly focused *reading instruction.* And her curriculum counters the parallel and evolving construction or reconstruction of young children as speakers and readers of English. A single-minded focus on early schooling in *English* ignores the existence of children like those in Ms. Yung's classroom, who are part of a notably increasing group in early education programs (August & Hakuta, 1997; Ballenger, 1999; Fassler, 2003).

Finally, the subject of our analyses, Ms. Yung's integrated curriculum, like the activity on Madlenka's block, is not offered here as an exemplar for readers to replicate. Every case is uniquely experienced by participants and uniquely bounded and theorized by researchers—who are sometimes also participants. So we offer Ms. Yung's curriculum as an example that is responsive to diverse learners and that challenges and complicates contemporary ways of constructing children, language, and literacy.

MRS. KAY'S CLASSROOM:
GENERALIZING ABOUT THE BASICS (ANNE)

Like Celia, I have been continuing on my case. Mrs. Kay's classroom is my entry point into "the imaginative universes" (Geertz, 1973, p. 13)—the experiential worlds—of children who are learning the standardized basics against the backdrop of these nonstandardized times of lively cultural, linguistic, and semiotic diversity. Among the literacy basics are those of grammatical usage, which I have featured in this book.

The slow piecework of analysis, described in Chapter 5, is yielding an evidentiary quilt, a written case that folds into its fabric details of talk, text, and action. These details construct and support propositional, past-tense assertions, or findings, about what was happening with the basics in Mrs. Kay's classroom. Among those assertions are these:

- The official basics were undergirded by an homogeneous and hierarchical notion of language: There were better ways of saying things that held across literacy practices.

- No child who spoke a marked nonstandard English variety "mastered"—used consistently in writing or even at all—grammatical features "fixed" in teacher-student editing conferences and whole-class sentence correction exercises.
- The children did reread and fix their sentences on their own initiative for syntactical sense, according to their existent grammar (i.e., so that the sentences would sound right to them).
- Children fixed their texts for reasons not formally included in the curriculum, specifically, for relational reasons. This sort of authorial reasoning was particularly evident when the composing event was situated within the social expectations and histories of unofficial relations and play practices.

Like the invented Liz and the actual Celia, I do not want to speak only of case-bound assertions. Rather, I aim to respond to the ongoing professional conversations about literacy "basics" for young children.

Discussion and Conclusion

To do so, in the discussion section of my case study, I need to move from the past tense of the above assertions to present tense assertions about the nature of my phenomenon—learning to write in a basics-oriented curriculum. This movement does not entail broad, sweeping statements, but a kind of "delicacy," as the ideas embedded in the details of a case are situated within issue-oriented dialogues (Geertz, 1973, p. 25).

Echoing Celia, in entering these dialogues, I do not want to reinforce a simplistic dichotomy between "basic" and "progressive" or "meaning-focused" language arts curricula. It would be all too easy to do so, especially since the beliefs and values about language (i.e., the language ideology) that undergirded the official basics in Mrs. Kay's room were evident as well in district, state, and federal documents on child literacy that informed classroom materials and teaching practices. In my discussion, though, I would note that classic writing pedagogy texts for young schoolchildren are silent on issues of language diversity and ideology. This silence may be in part a result of the singular role of children from middle-class, White communities in the initial formation of writing-process pedagogy (e.g., Graves, 1983). Matters of culture and language may have been inaudible in the data set.

In contrast, the children in Mrs. Kay's classroom were developing speakers of varied Englishes, among them African American Vernacular English and regional forms of nonstandard and standard English—all rule-governed systems of communication, products of social history and geography (Labov, 1972; Smitherman, 2000). Through their very voices, the children indexed their participation in a complex human society, with different cultural and linguistic resources.

Situating Mrs. Kay's classroom both within others' portraits of the cultural and linguistic diversity of American society and within the literature on child writing would help me to use my "small facts" to "speak to large issues" (Geertz, 1973, p. 23). Those small case-bound assertions help problematize dominant conceptions of writing "basics" as neutral conventions for encoding and organizing language in written graphics. In my discussion, those assertions would be rearticulated as assertions about learning to write itself:

- To encode, monitor, and edit written texts, children rely on what sounds right to them, that is, on familiar ways with words. In our linguistically complex society, what sounds "right" to young children will vary, not only for developmental reasons, but also for sociocultural ones.
- Young children's deliberate manipulation of language for rhetorical ends is dependent on opportunities to exercise agency in familiar social and communicative

events. In a linguistically diverse society, such rhetorical manipulations potentially include choices of language and vernaculars themselves.

In my discussion, I might borrow the following brief excerpt from a paper on the case of Mrs. Kay's class. In the excerpt, I am considering the implications of my findings, now situated in a larger conversation about grammatical usage:

> [T]he pedagogical point is not that children should not talk about, and have the opportunity to learn, the edited English of wider communication (Smitherman, Villanueva, & Canagrajah, 2003). Rather, I am pointing out, first, that "basic" matters of "usage" are complex developmental, social, cultural, and political matters. . . . Second, a curricular valuing and promoting of communicative flexibility, and the use of different language varieties as options and resources, seems critical. It matters in allowing children equal access to familiar voices [i.e., to "what sounds right"] as resources for learning to write. And it also matters in furthering socially, politically, and aesthetically sophisticated language use. As novelists and other verbal artists demonstrate, and ethnographers of communication in and out of the classroom document . . . [among them, Vasquez, Pease-Alvarez, & Shannon, 1994], such sophistication is necessary both to render and to participate widely within "a contradictory and multi-languaged world" (Bakhtin, 1981, p. 275). (Dyson, forthcoming)

As my discussion approaches its close, I imagine that I will focus in on that second point in the excerpt above, about communicative flexibility. This point is grounded in part in the case-bound assertion about children manipulating language for what can be deemed "horizontal," rather than hierarchical, reasons. That is, in making relational fix-its, children were manipulating their written language in order to manipulate, so to speak, unofficial peer relations, not to correctly follow a rule. (Readers may recall Lyron's concern with fixing Tionna's text to include Janette and Mandisa in the "boyfriend" play.) I would no doubt emphasize that, when engaging in play, the focal children manipulated the rhetorical and linguistic features of oral language to construct social relations (e.g., playing teacher and student, fast-food clerk and customer, and, of course, boyfriend and girlfriend[s]).

To establish the relevance of flexibility to issues of grammatical usage, I would situate the experiences of Mrs. Kay's children in the literature on child language development. Within that literature, there is no research support for the notion that explicit correction in and of itself is effective in eliminating features from a child's repertoire. There is evidence, though, that speakers of nondominant vernaculars must develop a kind of social and linguistic flexibility to meet the basic requirements of school, even though mastery, not flexibility, is the official goal.

For example, the literature on very young children's dialectical code-switching suggests that children develop such facility when given regular opportunities to exercise agency over using the vernacular in different social situations (see Clark, 2003, for review). And certainly young schoolchildren can explicitly acknowledge heritage dialects and languages through, for example, the study of multicultural literature that contains varied ways with words and related role play and other forms of drama (Delpit & Dowdy, 2002).

This discussion I am planning herein has its roots in my decision many months—and chapters—ago to visit schools in an urban district under pressure, like many others, to focus on "the basics." I did not turn away from those basics but delved into them by focusing in fine-grained ways on their enactment in a first-grade classroom. It was a humbling experience to be on the case in Mrs. Kay's room, experiencing how she and her lively children ventured into aspects of learning to write that no one—district consultants; federally approved authors of language arts guidebooks; nor myself, truth be told—had fully considered. From my very particular experience in Mrs. Kay's room, I am beginning, then, to turn toward the larger professional conversation and to newly fashion my case-bound assertions in its light. In this way I hope to add new understandings to the evolving dialogue about children, literacy, and schooling.

Beyond the Singular Case: On Blurring Our Own Boundaries

In our movement through these chapters between what happened in Ms. Yung's and Mrs. Kay's classrooms and what happens for children learning through language in our society, we are ultimately guided by a vision of a classroom in which Mrs. Kay's children and the slightly older peers of Ms. Yung's would be classmates. To support the children, the teacher would need to be guided by an understanding of learning to communicate, read, and write that would be expansive enough to incorporate our multilingual, multicultural population, yet specific enough to inform his or her own actions in a very particular situation, with very particular children taking up opportunities to learn—to exercise their agency—in their own distinctive ways. Living through classroom life with teachers and children in detail-rich case studies potentially stretches educators' experience in "naturalistic" ways beyond their own educational histories. And carefully constructed "propositions," in which the details of a case are situated within broader assertions about teaching and learning, potentially help synthesize these experiences so that common principles become salient. In these ways, we hope that the intellectual labor and joy of being on the case come to matter.

Suggestions for Further Reading

These sources, which we have referred to throughout the book, are rich in methodological detail. Readers may want to consult them for theoretical and practical guidance while carrying out their own studies.

Bogdan, R. C., & Biklen, S. K. (2003). *Qualitative research for education: An introduction to theories and methods* (4th ed.). New York: Allyn & Bacon.

The authors present a balance of theory, method, and real-life detail drawn from studies of educational practice and policy. Included in the textbook are brief updates on recent trends, for example, in practitioner research or the use of computer software for qualitative data analysis.

Corsaro, W. A. (2003). *"We're friends, right?" Inside kids' cultures.* Washington, DC: Joseph Henry Press.

This is not a book on methodology but, rather, one illustrating what Corsaro has learned about child cultures from his projects in American and Italian early education settings. Nonetheless, the book is helpful for our purposes due to the unusual detail Corsaro provides on his procedures for gaining access to, and becoming a participant in, children's worlds. He pays particular attention to the role of child talk in the construction of child cultures.

Emerson, R., Fretz, R., & Shaw, L. (1995). *Writing ethnographic fieldnotes.* Chicago: University of Chicago Press.

A well-detailed guide to the complexities of composing and using field notes. Using many examples of field notes, the authors discuss how such notes are composed from jottings, shaped by decisions about style and substance, move between description and reflection, and ultimately are reduced and reworked to develop a document: an ethnographic text. Contemporary issues, including the ethics of fieldwork, the reflexivity of the fieldworker, and the complexities of studying gender and race, are included.

Erickson, F. (1986). Qualitative methods in research on teaching. In M. S. Wittrock (Ed.), *Handbook of research on teaching* (3rd ed., pp. 119–161). New York: Macmillan.

A classic work on interpretive approaches to qualitative research, including sociolinguistic studies in classrooms. Erickson's insights on generalization are particularly illuminating.

Geertz, C. (1973). *The interpretation of cultures*. New York: Basic Books.
   This collection of essays by one of the foremost anthropologists
   of his generation goes to the heart of interpretive research. Concepts
   of multiple truths, local knowledge, culture as the making of meanings, among others, are richly rendered in this generative text. Geertz
   has been criticized by contemporary theorists for not attending to issues of power, but his basic insights remain central to interpretive
   research.
Graue, M. E., & Walsh, D. (1998). *Studying children in context: Theories,
   methods, and ethics*. Thousand Oaks, CA: Sage.
   A thoughtfully crafted text on carrying out research with children. The authors offer practical guidance, along with brief sections
   by other qualitative researchers, who present their personal takes
   and illustrations of aspects of the research process, for example, data
   analysis or the role of theory.
Kvale, S. (1996). *InterViews: An introduction to qualitative research interviewing*. Thousand Oaks, CA: Sage.
   A comprehensive guide to interviews as conversations that, according to the author, are "traveled" or "mined." Theoretical, methodological, and ethical issues are discussed within an interpretive framework, and practical guidelines are included throughout. A chapter on
   validity as a social construction and one addressing frequent objec-
   tions to interview research are especially thought-provoking.
Rosaldo, R. (1989). *Culture and truth: The remaking of social analysis*. Boston:
   Beacon Press.
   A richly theoretical and thoroughly engaging analysis of recent
   changes in talking about and studying culture. Using personal experience as well as key scholarly works, Rosaldo discusses the difficulty
   of treating cultures and their practices as self-contained wholes and of
   reducing individuals to singular cultural labels. At the same time, he
   illustrates how researchers' life experiences and collective identities
   (e.g., of race, gender, and class) can be the basis for analytic insights.
   Most important for our purposes, he emphasizes the value of situated
   case studies in countering assumptions of absolute human truths.
Strauss, A., & Corbin, J. (1998). *Basics of qualitative research: Grounded theory procedures and techniques* (2nd ed.). Newbury Park, CA: Sage.
   A demonstration of how one works with data to build theory
   from it (i.e., a theory grounded in analyzed data). Descriptions of
   open and focused (axial) coding give readers an understanding of
   the logic of coding as an analytic process. Some have found Strauss
   and Corbin's approach constraining, but the approach is meant to be
   used flexibly by researchers as they deem fit.

Illustrations of Case Studies

With an appreciation for the many published case studies that enhance our understandings of children, language, and literacy, we include book-length studies here that illustrate a range of cases, from *individual* as case to *transnational community* as case.

Finders, J. (1997). *Just girls: Hidden literacies and life in junior high*. New York: Teachers College Press.

A study of the literacy practices of two "friendship groups" of adolescent girls. Finders studied their literacy practices in and out of school, analyzing how those practices served to regulate and to enable their social performances as "popular girls" or "tough cookies." For example, the school activity of signing yearbooks was experienced very differently by the "popular girls," who counted the number of times their photos appeared, and by the "tough cookies," whose photos did not appear. Finders situates her cases within the economic circumstances and circulating ideologies (e.g., of the "developmental stage" of adolescence, of the nature of "good girls") in their common school and their distinctive familial cultures.

Fisherkeller, J. (2002). *Growing up with television: Everyday learning among young adolescents*. Philadelphia, PA: Temple University Press.

A study of middle school students watching, talking about, and critiquing television in their everyday lives. In some ways, Fisherkeller shared goals with Finders—to understand how young people make sense of themselves in contemporary times—but her methodology was very different. Her cases were not social groups but social *individuals*—in depth case studies of New York adolescents learning from and about television culture (i.e., television as a medium for the production of aesthetic, narrative, and ideological meaning). Similar to Finders, though, Fisherkeller's cases are not free-floating entities. Fisherkeller illustrates how young people's ways of using and learning from television were shaped by their economic circumstances and social situations at home, at school, with their peers, and in their anticipated futures.

Graue, M. E. (1993). *Ready for what? Constructing meanings of readiness for kindergarten*. Albany: State University of New York Press.

A study of school communities that encompassed children, school staff, and parents. Although Graue did not focus on language or literacy, she problematized the term *readiness*, a still-controversial term often tied to literacy, by investigating what readiness meant in three schools and the networks that intersected within them. The surrounding communities were White working-class, White middle-class, and Latino working-class; and each school community defined readiness differently. Thus, this was a case of construction of meanings that, in turn, led to particular constructions of children and the curriculum they were perceived to need.

Guerra, J. (1998). *Close to home: Oral and literate practices in a transnational Mexicano community.* New York: Teachers College Press.

An ethnography about border crossings, about a *transnational community* whose members participated in life in Mexican towns and Chicago, IL. Guerra questioned the reality of boundaries between countries and between what is conventionally called oral and literate behavior. Details of the participants' lives over a period of 9 years demonstrates how some communities cannot be accurately defined as "bounded" cases in terms of geography or ways of communicating.

Heath, S. B. (1983). *Ways with words: Language, life, and work in communities and classrooms.* New York: Cambridge University Press.

A groundbreaking 10-year study of three *cultural communities* that were close to each other geographically, yet culturally distinctive: a White working-class community, an African American working-class community, and a middle-class community. In Heath's ethnography of communication—her study of the communicative practices through which three social groups make meaning—she described in detail how her methods were tailored to suit the ways of these communities (e.g., no use of tape recorders initially), rather than how she actually collected and analyzed data. She was also in the vanguard of teacher research, as she enlisted teachers in the middle-class community to do ethnographic work and teach their students to do it as well.

Miller, P. (1982). *Amy, Wendy, and Beth: Learning language in South Baltimore.* Austin: University of Texas Press.

A study of children's language development in a White working-class community. The title of Miller's book suggests that these were case studies of individual children. A look at the rich transcriptions interspersed within, however, show that the case—the relevant social unit—was better defined as the children's families, including their mothers and extended family members who participated routinely in the language socialization process. Like an aspect of Heath's study, Miller's is a case of children's growing knowledge of the forms and uses of language—of local ways with words.

References

Allington, R. (2002). *Big Brother and the national reading curriculum: How ideology trumped evidence.* Portsmouth, NH: Heinemann.

Anderson, R., Hiebert, E., Scott, J., & Wilkinson, I. (1985). *Becoming a nation of readers.* Washington, DC: National Institute of Education.

Au, K. H., & Jordan, C. (1981). Teaching reading to Hawaiian children: Finding a culturally appropriate solution. In H. Trueba, G. P. Guthrie, & K. H. Au (Eds.), *Culture in the bilingual classroom: Studies in classroom ethnography* (pp. 139–152). Rowley, MA: Newberry House.

August, D., & Hakuta, K. (Eds.). (1997). *Improving schooling for language-minority children: A research agenda.* Washington, DC: National Research Council, National Academy Press.

Bakhtin, M. (1981). Discourse in the novel. In C. Emerson & M. Holquist (Eds.), *The dialogic imagination: Four essays by M. Bakhtin* (pp. 254–422). Austin: University of Texas Press.

Ballenger, C. (1999). *Teaching other people's children: Literacy and learning in a bilingual classroom.* New York: Teachers College Press.

Barton, D. (1994). *Literacy: An introduction to the ecology of written language.* London: Blackwell.

Basso, K. H. (1974). The ethnography of writing. In R. Bauman & J. Sherzer (Eds.), *Explorations in the ethnography of speaking* (pp. 425–432). Cambridge, England: Cambridge University Press.

Baylor, B., & Parnall, P. (1978). *The other way to listen.* New York: Simon & Schuster.

Becker, H. (1990). Generalizing from case studies. In E. Eisner & A. Peshkin (Eds.), *Qualitative inquiry in education: The continuing debate* (pp. 233–242). New York: Teachers College Press.

Bogdan, R. C., & Biklen, S. K. (2003). *Qualitative research for education: An introduction to theory and methods.* (4th ed.). Boston: Allyn & Bacon.

Bredekamp, S., & Copple, C. (Eds.). (1997). *Developmentally appropriate practice in early childhood programs* (Rev. ed.). Washington, DC: National Association for the Education of Young Children.

Brenna, S. (2003, November 9). The littlest test takers. *The New York Times,* pp. 32, 37.

Brown, M. W. (1976). *Goodnight, moon.* New York: Harper Collins.

Carrasco, R., Vera, A., & Cazden, C. (1981). Aspects of bilingual student's communicative competence in the classroom: A case study. In R. Duran (Ed.), *Latino language and communicative behavior* (pp. 237–269). Norwood, NJ: Ablex.

Cazden, C. (2001). *Classroom discourse: The language of teaching and learning.* (2nd ed.). Portsmouth, NH: Heinemann.

Cazden, C., John, V., & Hymes, D. (Eds.). (1972). *Functions of language in the classroom.* New York: Teachers College Press.

Chittenden, E., Salinger, T., & Bussis, A. (2001). *Inquiry into meaning: An investigation of learning to read* (Rev. ed.). New York: Teachers College Press.

Clandinin, D. J., & Connelly, F. M. (2000). *Narrative inquiry: Experience and story in qualitative research.* San Francisco: Jossey-Bass.

Clark, E. V. (2003). *First language acquisition.* Cambridge, England: Cambridge University Press.

Clifford, J., & Marcus, G. E. (Eds.) . (1986). *Writing culture: The poetics and politics of ethnography.* Berkeley: University of California Press.

Cochran-Smith, M. (2004). Taking stock in 2004: Teacher education in dangerous times. *Journal of Teacher Education, 55*(1), 3–7.

Corsaro, W. (1981). Entering the child's world: Research strategies for field entry and data collection in a preschool setting. In J. Green & C. Wallat (Eds.), *Ethnography and language in educational settings* (pp. 117–146). Norwood, NJ: Ablex.

Corsaro, W. A. (2003). *"We're friends, right?" Inside kids' cultures.* Washington, DC: Joseph Henry Press.

Delgado Bernal, D. (1998). Using a Chicana feminist epistemology in educational research. *Harvard Educational Review, 68*, 555–582.

Delpit, L., & Dowdy, J. K. (Eds.). (2002). *The skin that we speak: Thoughts on language and culture in the classroom.* New York: The New Press.

Denzin, N. K., & Lincoln, Y. S. (Eds.). (2000). *Handbook of qualitative research.* (2nd ed.). Thousand Oaks, CA: Sage.

Diaz, S., Moll, L. C., & Mehan, H. (1986). Sociocultural resources in instruction: A context-specific approach. In California State Department Bilingual Education Office (Ed.), *Beyond language: Social and cultural factors in schooling language minority students* (pp. 187–230). Los Angeles: Evaluation, Dissemination, and Assessment Center.

Duranti, A., & Goodwin, C. (Eds.). (1992). *Rethinking context: Language as an interactive phenomenon.* New York: Cambridge University Press.

Dyson, A. Haas. (1984). Learning to write/Learning to do school: Emergent writers' interpretations of school literacy tasks. *Research in the Teaching of English, 18*, 233–264.

Dyson, A. Haas. (1993). *Social worlds of children learning to write in an urban primary school.* New York: Teachers College Press.

Dyson, A. Haas. (1997). *Writing superheroes: Contemporary childhood, popular culture, and classroom literacy.* New York: Teachers College Press.

Dyson, A. Haas. (1999). Transforming transfer: Unruly children, contrary texts, and the persistence of the pedagogical order. In A. Iran-Nejad & P. D. Pearson (Eds.), *Review of research in education: Vol. 24 (pp. 141–171).* Washington, DC: American Educational Research Association.

Dyson, A. Haas. (2003). *The brothers and sisters learn to write: Popular literacies in childhood and school cultures.* New York: Teachers College Press.

Dyson, A. Haas. (forthcoming). Literacy "basics" in childhood spaces: A critical perspective on the "basics." Paper prepared for Conference on Critical Issues in Early Literacy Development, University of Arizona, Tucson. In Y. M. Goodman (Ed.), *Critical issues in early literacy development.*

Emerson, R., Fretz, R., & Shaw, L. (1995). *Writing ethnographic fieldnotes.* Chicago: University of Chicago Press.

Erickson, F. (1986). Qualitative methods in research on teaching. In M. Wittrock (Ed.), *Handbook of research on teaching* (3rd ed., pp. 119–161). Washington, DC: American Educational Research Association.

Erickson, F. (2002). Culture and human development. *Human Development, 45*, 299–306.

Fassler, R. (2003). *Room for talk: Teaching and learning in a multilingual kindergarten.* New York: Teachers College Press.

Feld, S., & Basso, K. H. (Eds.). (1996). *Senses of place.* Santa Fe, NM: School of American Research Press.

Finders, M. J. (1997). *Just girls: Hidden literacies and life in junior high.* New York: Teachers College Press.

Fontana, A., & Frey, J. H. (2000). The interview: From structured questions to negotiated text. In N. K. Denzin & Y. S. Lincoln (Eds.), *Handbook of qualitative research* (2nd ed., pp. 645–672). Thousand Oaks, CA: Sage.

Foucault, M. (1978). *The history of sexuality.* New York: Pantheon.

Foucault, M. (1980). *Language, counter-memory, practice: Selected essays and interviews.* Ithaca, NY: Cornell University Press.

Foucault, M. (1981). The order of discourse. In R. Young (Ed.), *Untying the text: A poststructuralist reader* (pp. 48–78). Boston: Routledge & Kegan Paul.

Garan, E. (2002). *Resisting reading mandates: How to triumph with the truth.* Portsmouth, NH: Heinemann.

Geertz, C. (1973). *The interpretation of cultures.* New York: Basic Books.

Geertz, C. (1995). *After the fact: Two countries, four decades, one anthropologist.* Cambridge, MA: Harvard University Press.

Geertz, C. (1996). Afterword. In S. Feld & K. H. Basso (Eds.), *Sense of place* (pp. 259–262). Santa Fe, NM: School of American Research Press.

Genishi, C. (1996, April). *Research on/with children and teachers: Revealing stories of difference.* Paper presented at the annual meeting of the American Educational Research Association, New York, NY.

Genishi, C., Dubetz, N., & Focarino, C. (1995). Reconceptualizing theory through practice: Insights from a first-grade teacher and second-language theorists. In S. Reifel (Ed.), *Advances in early education and day care* (vol. 7, pp. 123–152). Greenwich, CT: JAI Press.

Genishi, C., Stires, S., & Yung-Chan, D. (2001). Writing in an integrated curriculum: Pre-Kindergarten English language learners as symbol-makers. *Elementary School Journal, 101,* 399–416.

Genishi, C., Yung-Chan, D., & Stires, S. (2000). Talking their way into print: English language learners in a pre-kindergarten classroom. In D. S. Strickland & L. M. Morrow (Eds.), *Beginning reading and writing* (pp. 66–80). New York: Teachers College Press.

Gilroy, P. (1997). Diaspora and the detours of identity. In K. Woodward (Ed.), *Identity and difference* (pp. 299–346). London: The Open University and Sage.

Glaser, B. G., & Strauss, A. L. (1967). *The discovery of grounded theory: Strategies for qualitative research.* Chicago: Aldine.

Goodwin, C. & Duranti, A. (1992). Rethinking context: An introduction. In A. Duranti & C. Goodwin (Eds.), *Rethinking context: Language as an interactive phenomenon* (pp. 1–46). New York: Cambridge University Press.

Graue, M. E., & Walsh, D. J. (Eds.). (1998). *Studying children in context: Theories, methods, and ethics.* Thousand Oaks, CA: Sage.

Graves, D. (1973). *Children's writing: Research directions and hypotheses based upon an examination of the writing process of seven-year-old children.* Unpublished doctoral dissertation, State University of New York, Buffalo.

Graves, D. H. (1983). *Writing: Teachers and children at work.* Portsmouth, NH: Heinemann Educational Books.

Gubrium, J. F., & Holstein, J. A. (2002). *Handbook of interview research: Context and method.* Thousand Oaks, CA: Sage.

Gupta, A., & Ferguson, J. (1997). Beyond "culture": Space, identity, and the politics of difference. In A. Gupta & J. Ferguson (Eds.), *Culture, power, place: Explorations in critical anthropology* (pp. 33–51). Durham, NC: Duke University Press.

Hall, S. (Ed.). (1997). *Representation: Cultural representations and signifying practices.* London: Sage.

Hanks, W. F. (1996). *Language and communicative practices.* Boulder, CO: Westview Press.

Head Start Bureau. (2003). *Head Start National Reporting System on Child Outcomes.* Retrieved August 4, 2004, from http://www.headstartinfo.org/publications/im03/im03_07.htm

Heath, S. B. (1982). Questioning at home and at school: A comparative study. In G. Spindler (Ed.), *Doing the ethnography of schooling* (pp. 96–101). New York: Holt, Rinehart, & Winston.

Heath, S. B. (1983). *Ways with words: Language, life, and work in communities and classrooms.* Cambridge, England: Cambridge University Press.

Hohmann, M., Banet, B., & Weikart, D. P. (1979). *Young children in action: A manual for preschool educators.* Ypsilanti, MI: High/Scope Educational Research Foundation.

Hymes, D. (1972a). Models of the interaction of language and social life. In J. J. Gumperz & D. Hymes (Eds.), *Directions in sociolinguistics* (pp. 35–71). New York: Holt, Rinehart & Winston.

Hymes, D. (1972b). On communicative competence. In J. Pride & J. Holmes (Eds.), *Sociolinguistics: Selected readings* (pp. 269–293). Harmondsworth, U.K.: Penguin.

Hymes, D. (1972c). Introduction. In C. Cazden, D. Hymes, & V. John (Eds.), *Functions of language in the classroom.* (pp. xi–lvii) New York: Teachers College Press.

International Reading Association. (2001). *Second language literacy instruction: A position statement of the International Reading Association.* [Brochure]. Newark, DE: Author.

Jacob, E., & White, S. (Eds.) (2002). Scientific research in education. [Special issue]. *Educational Researcher, 31*(8).

Knight, M., Bentley, C. C., Norton, N. E. L., & Dixon, I. R. (2004). (De)constructing (in)visible parent/guardian consent forms: Negotiating power, reflexivity and the collective within qualitative research. *Qualitative Inquiry, 10,* 390–411.

Kvale, S. (1996). *InterViews: An introduction to qualitative research interviewing.* Thousand Oaks, CA: Sage.

Labov, W. (1972). *Language in the inner city.* Philadelphia: University of Pennsylvania Press.

Lewin, T. (1999, September 6). No more fun and games as children go back to school. *New York Times,* p. A-1.

McDermott, R. P. (1987). The explanation of minority school failure, again. *Anthropology and Education Quarterly, 18,* 361–364.

Mehan, H. (1982). The structure of classroom events and their consequences for student performance. In P. Gilmore & A. A. Glatthorn (Eds.), *Children in and out of school* (pp. 59–87). Washington, DC: Center for Applied Linguistics.

Merriam, S. B. (2001). *Qualitative research and case study applications in education.* San Francisco: Jossey-Bass.

Meyer, C. A., Klein, E. L., & Genishi, C. (1994). Peer relationships among four preschool second language learners in "small group time." *Early Childhood Research Quarterly, 9,* 61–85.

Miller, P., & Goodnow, J. J. (1995). Cultural practices: Toward an integration of culture and development. In J. J. Goodnow, P. J. Miller, & F. Kessel (Eds.), *Cultural practices as contexts for development, No. 67, New directions in child development* (pp. 5–16). San Francisco: Jossey-Bass.

Mishler, E. G. (1986). *Research interviewing: Context and narrative.* Cambridge, MA: Harvard University Press.

Moll, L. C. (1992). Bilingual classroom studies and community analysis: Some recent trends. *Educational Researcher, 21*(2), 20–24.

Moll, L. C., & Diaz, D. (1987). Change as the goal of educational research. *Anthropology and Education Quarterly, 18,* 300–311.

Ochs, E. (1979). Transcription as theory. In E. Ochs & B. B. Schieffelin (Eds.), *Developmental pragmatics* (pp. 43–72). New York: Academic.

Ortner, S. (1996). *Making gender: The politics and erotics of culture.* Boston: Beacon Press.

Ortner, S. (1999). Introduction. In S. Ortner (Ed.), *The fate of "culture": Geertz and beyond.* Berkeley: University of California Press.

Padden, C., & Humphries, T. (1988). *Deaf in America: Voices from a culture.* Cambridge, MA: Harvard University Press.

Paley, V. G. (1981). *Wally's stories.* Cambridge, MA: Harvard University Press.

Perkins, A. (1998). *Hand, hand, fingers, thumb.* New York: Random House Children's Books.

Philips, S. (1972). Participant structures and communicative competence: Warm Springs children in community and classroom. In C. B. Cazden, V. P. John, & D. Hymes (Eds.), *The functions of language in the classroom* (pp. 370–394). New York: Teachers College Press.

Philips, S. (1975). Literacy as a mode of communication on the Warm Springs Indian Reservation. In E. H. Lenneberg & E. Lenneberg (Eds.), *Foundations of language development* (pp. 367–381). New York: Academic Press and Paris: UNESCO.

Ramsey, C. (1997). *Deaf children in public schools.* Washington, DC: Gallaudet University Press.

Reyes, M. de la Luz. (1992). Challenging venerable assumptions: Literacy instruction for linguistically different students. *Harvard Educational Review, 62,* 427–446.

Richardson, L. (1990). *Writing strategies: Reaching diverse audiences.* Newbury Park, CA: Sage.

Rosaldo, R. (1989). *Culture and truth: The remaking of social analysis.* Boston: Beacon Press.

Sanjek, R. (Ed.). (1990). *Fieldnotes: The makings of anthropology.* Ithaca, NY: Cornell University Press.

Seidman, I. E. (1991). *Interviewing as qualitative research: A guide for researchers in education and the social sciences.* New York: Teachers College Press.

Sis, P. (2000). *Madlenka.* New York: Farrar, Straus, Giroux.

Smitherman, G. (2000). *Talkin that talk: Language, culture, and education in African America.* New York: Routledge.

Smitherman, G., Villanueva, V., & Canagarajah, S. (Eds.). (2003). *Language diversity in the classroom: From intention to practice.* Carbondale: Southern Illinois University Press.

Snow, C., Burns, S., & Griffin, P. (Eds.). (1998). *Preventing reading difficulties in young children.* Washington, DC: National Academy Press.

Stake, R. E. (1995). *The art of case study research.* Thousand Oaks, CA: Sage.

Strauss, A., & Corbin, J. (1990). *Basics of qualitative research: Grounded theory procedures and techniques.* Newbury Park, CA: Sage.

Thorne, B. (1993). *Gender play: Girls and boys in school.* New Brunswick, NJ: Rutgers University Press.

U.S. Department of Education, National Center for Education Statistics. (2003). *Overview of public elementary and secondary schools and districts: School year 2001–2002* (NCES 2003–411). Washington, DC: Author.

Vasquez, O., Pease-Alvarez, L., & Shannon, S. (1994). *Pushing boundaries: Language and culture in a Mexicano community.* New York: Cambridge University Press.

Vygotsky, L. S. (1962). *Thought and language.* Cambridge, MA: MIT Press.

Watson-Gegeo, K. (1988). Ethnography in ESL: Defining the essentials. *TESOL Quarterly, 22,* 575–592.

Weis, L., & Fine, M. (Eds.). (2000). *Speed bumps: A student-friendly guide to qualitative research.* New York: Teachers College Press.

Wolf, M. (1992). *A thrice told tale: Feminism, postmodernism, and ethnographic responsibility.* Stanford, CA: Stanford University Press.

Yung-Chan, D., Stires, S., & Genishi, C. (1997). *Learning the words of our language: Experience and expansion in pre-kindergarten.* Proposal submitted to Spencer Foundation Practitioner Research Communication and Mentoring Grant Program.

Zentella, A. C. (1997). *Growing up bilingual: Puerto Rican children in New York.* New York: Blackwell.

Index

About the Authors

Anne Haas Dyson is a former teacher of young children and is currently a professor of education at Michigan State University, where she teaches courses related to qualitative research methods and language and literacy education. Previously, she was on the faculty of the University of Georgia and the University of California at Berkeley, where she was a recipient of the University of California at Berkeley's Distinguished Teaching Award. She studies the social lives and literacy learning of schoolchildren. Among her publications are *Multiple Worlds of Child Writers: Friends Learning to Write; Social Worlds of Children Learning to Write in an Urban Primary School*, which was awarded NCTE's David Russell Award for Distinguished Research; *Writing Superheroes: Contemporary Childhood, Popular Culture, and Classroom Literacy*; and *The Brothers and Sisters Learn to Write: Popular Literacies in Childhood and School Cultures*.

Celia Genishi is professor of education and coordinator of the program in early childhood education in the Department of Curriculum and Teaching at Teachers College, Columbia University. She is a former secondary Spanish and preschool teacher and now teaches courses related to early childhood education and qualitative research methods. Previously, she was on the faculty at the University of Texas at Austin and Ohio State University. She is coauthor of both *Language Assessment in the Early Years* and *Ways of Studying Children*, is editor of *Ways of Assessing Children*, and is co-editor of *The Need for Story: Cultural Diversity in Classroom and Community*. Her research interests include collaborative research with teachers on alternative assessments, childhood bilingualism, and language use in classrooms. She is a recipient of the Advocate for Justice Award, given by the American Association for Colleges of Teacher Education.